The American Testament

THE AMERICAN TESTAMENT

Mortimer J. Adler
and
William Gorman

for the Institute for Philosophical Research
and
the Aspen Institute for Humanistic Studies

PRAEGER PUBLISHERS

NEW YORK

Published in the United States of America in 1975
by Praeger Publishers, Inc.
111 Fourth Avenue, New York, N.Y. 10003

© 1975 by Praeger Publishers, Inc.

"The Gettysburg Address" appeared originally in *The New Yorker,*
© 1975 The New Yorker Magazine, Inc.

Library of Congress Cataloging in Publication Data

Adler, Mortimer Jerome, 1902–
   The American testament.

   Includes index.
      1. United States. Declaration of Independence.   2. United States.
Constitution.   3. Lincoln, Abraham, Pres. U.S., 1809–1865. Gettysburg
address.   4. Civil rights—United States.   I. Gorman, William, joint au-
thor.   II. San Francisco. Institute for Philosophical Research.   III. Aspen
Institute for Humanistic Studies.   IV. Title.
E221.A46   973.3'13   75-3618
ISBN 0-275-34060-0

Printed in the United States of America

Contents

5

Preface

————— ◆•◆• —————

WE are grateful to the Aspen Institute for Humanistic Studies and to Joseph Slater and John Hunt, its President and Vice-President, for the auspices of the conference that was preparatory to the writing of this book. We wish to express our appreciation for the contributions made by the participants in that conference, held in Aspen, Colorado, on July 7–9, 1974.

The participants included Dumas Malone, Professor Emeritus of History at the University of Virginia and the biographer of Jefferson; Edward H. Levi, then President of the University of Chicago and now Attorney General of the United States; James F. Hoge, Jr., Editor of the Chicago *Sun Times;* Seymour Topping, Assistant Managing Editor of the *New York Times;* William Moyers of Station WNET, New York; Sidney Hyman, Professor of Criminal Justice at the University of Illinois in Chicago; Douglass Cater, Director of the Aspen Institute Program on Communications and Society; Phillips Talbot, President of the Asia Society; C. A. Shillinglaw, Senior Vice-President of the Coca-Cola Company; Father Jerome B. Coll, S.J., of the Regis Educational Corporation; James F. Henry, President of the Edna McConnell Clark Foundation; Mary Morrisett, New York City; Alvin I. Brown, President of the Aldon Construction Company of Washington, D.C.; Bethuel M. Webster of Webster Sheffield Fleischmann Hitchcock & Brookfield in New York City; and Elizabeth Paepcke, Trustee of the Aspen Institute.

Both in the preparation of the original draft of the materials that were submitted to the Aspen Conference and also in the preparation of the manuscript of this book, we received guidance and assistance

7

from our colleagues at the Institute for Philosophical Research. We wish to acknowledge specifically the contributions made by Otto Bird, Charles Van Doren, and John Van Doren. We also wish to express our appreciation to Marlys Buswell of the Institute staff for her painstaking editorial work on the manuscript.

We have tried to keep footnotes to a minimum. Information about persons, places, and events connected with the documents is given in a glossary at the end of the book. We are grateful to Wayne Moquin for his assistance in preparing this glossary.

In the textual passages that we have quoted, we have here and there introduced italicization for emphasis.

MJA
WG

Introduction

LOOKING toward the bicentennial anniversary of the United States of America, the Aspen Institute for Humanistic Studies held a three-day conference in July 1974 to consider the significance of three historic statements of the American idea—the Declaration of Independence, the Preamble to the Constitution, and the Gettysburg Address.

Collaborating with the Aspen Institute on this occasion, the Institute for Philosophical Research proposed that the three documents be regarded as the "American Testament," and it prepared commentaries on them to guide the discussion in Aspen. The authors of this book, Mortimer Adler and William Gorman, served as moderators of the conference. At the conclusion of the conference, the participants recommended that the commentaries on the documents constituting the American Testament be revised in the light of the discussion and prepared for publication. Mr. Gorman, who prepared the original draft of the commentaries, revised and expanded that draft, which went through further expansions and revisions to become this book.

The proposal that the Declaration of Independence, the Preamble to the Constitution, and the Gettysburg Address be regarded as the American Testament arose from the following considerations. To an astonishing and unprecedented degree, the United States was born out of sustained argument and grave political deliberation which committed this nation to a coherent political doctrine. That doctrine is set forth with an inspired brevity in a few momentous state papers—the first occurring at the moment of this country's resolution for independence, the second at the moment of the new government's formation, and the third at the moment of the major crisis in our national history. Direct and concentrated inquiry into the truth of that doctrine should be a steady part of the American experience, and the basic propositions in it should be the object of sustained, disciplined public discussion, not only during the bicentennial celebration, but at all times.

To regard the three documents chosen for this purpose as constituting a *testament* attributes to them a character that calls for a special mode of interpretation—the kind of interpretation that the faithful give to scriptures they look upon as sacred. The assumption underlying the way in which Muslims read the Koran, Jews the Old Testament, and Christians the New Testament is that the text they are reading contains truths which they should make the most strenuous effort to discover by patient and careful exegesis. Such a reading is called "exegetical" because it tries "to lead out of" the text the truth assumed to be in it.

To approach the three documents that constitute the American Testament in this way does not require us to regard them as sacred scriptures or as revealed truth, nor indeed as the basis for any sort of "civil religion." There is a long tradition of commentary on secular writings in which the approach to the text being interpreted is analogous to the approach of the faithful to sacred texts. Medieval commentaries on the works of Plato and Aristotle—by Arabic, Jewish, and Christian teachers—can be cited as examples of this method of reading a text for the purpose of discovering the truth it is supposed to contain. Modern examples are to be found in the extensive commentaries on the writings of Immanuel Kant or Karl Marx.

With some variation in style, what is common to all these examples of exegetical reading, whether of secular texts or of texts regarded as sacred, is a method of interpretation that concentrates on the meaning of words, phrases, and sentences, and on the relation between one element in the discourse and another, while paying little or no attention to contextual considerations or to psychological and sociological factors that may or may not have been responsible for the genesis of the texts being interpreted. An exegetical reading is concerned with philological aspects of the text, with the biography of its author, or with the historical circumstances under which it appeared *only* to the extent that these considerations contribute to an understanding of the text, not as affecting judgments about the truth of what is being said.

In sharp contrast to the exegetical method of reading a text is another method of commentary, which was called "the higher criticism" when, in the nineteenth century, it was first applied to the Old and the New Testaments. This method of interpretation is widely prevalent today, especially in the reading of political documents such as the ones chosen to be components of the American Testament. It makes little or no effort to get at the truth that the text being commented on may contain; it may almost be said to have no concern with the truth or falsity of what is being said *in* the document under consideration. Instead, the truth with which it is concerned is the truth *about* the document in question. To this end, it concentrates on the historical circumstances, the sociological influences, and the psychological motivations that are thought to have determined its content.

These two methods of interpreting and commenting on the written word are thus seen to differ radically with respect to the truth with which they are concerned—the one with the truth *in* the document, the other with the truth *about* the document. This book offers its readers one approach to the three documents that are the subject of its three commentaries—the approach that has been called an exegetical reading of them. This by no means precludes the other approach, but it does require the reader to accept, even if only provisionally, the assumption underlying the approach made here; namely, that the three documents under consideration contain basic truths to be ferreted out by the most careful explication of the meaning implicit in the words of the text. On this assumption, the effort of the commentator—and of the reader as well—should be to arrive at as clear and explicit a statement of these truths as can be found.

The interpretations by the exegetical method that this book advances can be challenged in at least two ways. One way is to question the accuracy or soundness of the interpretation being advanced; to be effective, such a challenge should be accompanied by the use of the same method to produce another, somewhat divergent interpretation. A second way, which would accept the interpretations here offered as correct, is to question the validity of the propositions that the commentary claims to be the basic truths contained in the documents. Here it is not the meaning of the document that is in question, but rather the truth of what the document is interpreted as meaning.

This book will fail in its purpose to arouse a sustained, critical discussion of the American idea if its readers do not challenge it in one or another of these ways; but, in doing so, the readers must also discharge the intellectual obligations attached to the questions they raise—to provide an alternative exegesis, in the one case, and to provide a refutation based on relevant and cogent reasons, in the other.

It was said above that the exegetical approach to an important text or document does not preclude the quite opposite approach that is concerned with the truth *about* the document rather than with the truth *in* it. The reverse must also be said, because it may be mistakenly thought that what can be found out about a document's historical origins, about its surrounding circumstances, or about the motivations of its writer or writers precludes an attempt to find out the meaning inherent in the statements it makes and to say whether or not what they mean is true. That is certainly not the case; nor is it even correct to think that the interpretation arrived at by an exegetical reading should be affected, colored, or slanted in any essential way by whatever facts can be discovered about the document's historical background, circumstantial setting, or psychological genesis.

There is one other misapprehension to which attention should be called in order to ensure its avoidance. To claim that this or any other exegetical reading of the three documents comprised by the American Testament has discovered a political doctrine that is not only significant and coherent but also true does not involve making the further claim that Americans over the last two centuries have lived up to the truth of the doctrine to which they have, from time to time, given verbal expressions of loyalty. They may do precisely that—yet only that—even more vociferously during this bicentennial period.

This book does not dwell on the discrepancies between the truths it holds up for scrutiny and the actual practice of the citizens of this country or the performance of its government. Just mention of the fact should suffice to call to mind how often the actions of Americans and of their government, both past and present, have departed from or traversed those truths.

Nor does this book give more than passing notice to the fact that the truths to which it tries to call attention are not universally acknowledged, either in America or in the world. In this connection, special mention should be made of the truth about the specific nature of man, on which human equality rests, and the truth about the natural rights of man, equally inherent in all men, which provide the indispensable criteria of political, economic, and social justice, as well as the basis for claiming that democracy is the only perfectly just form of government.

The American Testament

The Declaration of Independence

WHEN, IN THE COURSE OF HUMAN EVENTS, it becomes necessary for one people to dissolve the political bands which have connected them with another, and to assume, among the powers of the earth, the separate and equal station to which the laws of nature and of nature's God entitle them, a decent respect to the opinions of mankind requires that they should declare the causes which impel them to the separation.

We hold these truths to be self-evident, that all men are created equal; that they are endowed by their Creator with certain unalienable rights; that among these are life, liberty, and the pursuit of happiness. That, to secure these rights, governments are instituted among men, deriving their just powers from the consent of the governed; that, whenever any form of government becomes destructive of these ends, it is the right of the people to alter or to abolish it, and to institute a new government, laying its foundation on such principles, and organizing its powers in such form, as to them shall seem most likely to effect their safety and happiness. Prudence, indeed, will dictate that governments long established should not be changed for light and transient causes; and, accordingly, all experience hath shown, that mankind are more disposed to suffer, while evils are sufferable, than to right themselves by abolishing the forms to which they are accustomed. But, when a long train of abuses and usurpations, pursuing invariably the same object, evinces a design to reduce them under absolute despotism, it is their right, it is their duty, to throw off such government, and to provide new guards for their future security. Such has been the patient sufferance of these colonies, and such is now the necessity which constrains them to alter their former systems of government. The history of the present King of Great Britain is a history of repeated injuries and usurpations, all having, in direct object, the establishment of an absolute tyranny over these states. To prove this, let facts be submitted to a candid world:

He has refused his assent to laws the most wholesome and necessary for the public good.

He has forbidden his governors to pass laws of immediate and pressing importance, unless suspended in their operation till his assent should be obtained; and, when so suspended, he has utterly neglected to attend to them.

He has refused to pass other laws for the accommodation of large districts of people, unless those people would relinquish the right of representation in the legislature; a right inestimable to them, and formidable to tyrants only.

He has called together legislative bodies at places unusual, uncomfortable, and distant from the depository of their public records, for the sole purpose of fatiguing them into compliance with his measures.

He has dissolved representative houses repeatedly, for opposing, with manly firmness, his invasions on the rights of the people.

He has refused, for a long time after such dissolutions, to cause others to be elected; whereby the legislative powers, incapable of annihilation, have returned to the people at large for their exercise; the state remaining, in the meantime, exposed to all the danger of invasion from without, and convulsions within.

He has endeavored to prevent the population of these States; for that purpose, obstructing the laws for naturalization of foreigners, refusing to pass others to encourage their migration hither, and raising the conditions of new appropriations of lands.

He has obstructed the administration of justice, by refusing his assent to laws for establishing judiciary powers.

He has made judges dependent on his will alone, for the tenure of their offices, and the amount and payment of their salaries.

He has erected a multitude of new offices, and sent hither swarms of officers to harass our people, and eat out their substance.

He has kept among us, in time of peace, standing armies, without the consent of our legislatures.

He has affected to render the military independent of, and superior to, the civil power.

He has combined, with others, to subject us to a jurisdiction foreign to our Constitution, and unacknowledged by our laws; giving his assent to their acts of pretended legislation:

For quartering large bodies of armed troops among us:

For protecting them by a mock trial, from punishment, for any murders which they should commit on the inhabitants of these States:

For cutting off our trade with all parts of the world:

For imposing taxes on us without our consent:

For depriving us, in many cases, of the benefit of trial by jury:

For transporting us beyond seas to be tried for pretended offenses:

For abolishing the free system of English laws in a neighboring province, establishing therein an arbitrary government, and enlarging its boundaries, so as to render it at once an example and fit instrument for introducing the same absolute rule into these colonies:

For taking away our charters, abolishing our most valuable laws, and altering, fundamentally, the forms of our governments:

For suspending our own legislatures, and declaring themselves invested with power to legislate for us in all cases whatsoever.

He has abdicated government here, by declaring us out of his protection, and waging war against us.

He has plundered our seas, ravaged our coasts, burnt our towns, and destroyed the lives of our people.

He is, at this time, transporting large armies of foreign mercenaries to complete the works of death, desolation, and tyranny, already begun, with circumstances of cruelty and perfidy scarcely paralleled in the most barbarous ages, and totally unworthy the head of a civilized nation.

He has constrained our fellow citizens, taken captive on the high seas, to bear arms against their country, to become the executioners of their friends and brethren, or to fall themselves by their hands.

He has excited domestic insurrections amongst us, and has endeavored to bring on the inhabitants of our frontiers, the merciless Indian savages, whose known rule of warfare is an undistinguished destruction of all ages, sexes, and conditions.

In every stage of these oppressions, we have petitioned for redress, in the most humble terms; our repeated petitions have been answered only by repeated injury. A prince, whose character is thus marked by every act which may define a tyrant, is unfit to be the ruler of a free people.

Nor have we been wanting in attention to our British brethren. We have warned them, from time to time, of attempts by their legislature to extend an unwarrantable jurisdiction over us. We have reminded them of the circumstances of our emigration and settlement here. We have appealed to their native justice and magnanimity, and we have conjured them, by the ties of our common kindred, to disavow these usurpations, which would inevitably interrupt our connections and correspondence. They, too, have been deaf to the voice of justice and consanguinity. We must, therefore, acquiesce in the necessity which denounces our separation, and hold them, as we hold the rest of mankind, enemies in war, in peace, friends.

We, therefore, the representatives of the united States of America, in general Congress assembled, appealing to the Supreme Judge of the world for the rectitude of our intentions, do, in the name, and by the authority of the good people of these colonies, solemnly publish and declare, that these united colonies are, and of right ought to be, free and independent states; that they are absolved from all allegiance to the British Crown, and that all political connection between them and the state of Great Britain is, and ought to be, totally dissolved; and that, as free and independent states, they have full power to levy war, conclude peace, contract alliances, establish commerce, and to do all other acts and things which independent states may of right do. And, for the support of this declaration, with a firm reliance on the protection of Divine Providence, we mutually pledge to each other our lives, our fortunes, and our sacred honor.

The Declaration of Independence

All honor to Jefferson—to the man who, in
the concrete pressure of a struggle for national
independence by a single people, had the cool-
ness, forecast, and capacity to introduce into a
merely revolutionary document, an abstract
truth, applicable to all men and all times, and
so to embalm it there that today and in all
coming days it shall be a rebuke . . . to the very
harbingers of re-appearing tyranny.
ABRAHAM LINCOLN, 1859

THE four-part structure of the Declaration of Independence is
lucid. In the first part, the Declaration sets forth broadly the nature
and intent of the action taken in Congress on July 2 with the passage of a Resolution of Independence and the reason for addressing
a universal audience concerning that action. The second part presents the theory that provides the basis for a right to revolution and
delineates the kind of factual situation that would make the exercise
of that right a duty. The third part affirms that such a factual situation exists. In the fourth part, it is solemnly declared that the right
is being exercised.

When, in the course of human events, it becomes
necessary for one people to dissolve the political
bands which have connected them with another,
and to assume, among the powers of the earth, the
separate and equal station to which the laws of
nature and of nature's God entitle them, a decent

21

respect to the opinions of mankind requires that
they should declare the causes which impel them to
the separation.

This one-sentence paragraph is complex. But the basic proposition asserted is this: *The causes of a revolutionary action should be
declared.*

Why is this the case? To whom should the declaration be made?
The phrases and clauses of the complex sentence answer such
questions. As they do so, they reveal some important points of
doctrine.

A revolutionary act, dissolving prior political bonds, abolishing
the prior form of government, can and should be a fully human
act, an act of deliberative and prudent will, an act in the moral
order. As such, it is of interest to the universal audience. It is of
concern in the court of reason—of concern to the powers of the
earth, constituted as a community of nations, however loosely, by
respect for those opinions and judgments that are decisive for the
life of that community. Decent respect, then, for the opinions of
mankind requires that a candidate for separate and equal station
among the powers of the earth should make a candid declaration
to a candid world.

The Declaration was not to be made to Great Britain. The time
for constitutional arguments and for petitions had passed. The
Declaration had to be what Jefferson later called it, "an appeal to
the tribunal of the world." Evoking such a tribunal involves what
might be called an aspirational affirmation. Jefferson and the
signers were widely read students of human history, firmly aware
of the play in history of irrational, arbitrary forces. Their affirmation that human history should be taken as something in the moral
order was made despite, not in ignorance of, the general turgid
course of that history.

Some diction in the first lines of the Declaration underlines the
conviction that the Americans understood themselves as acting in
the moral order, in which judgments of right and wrong are
applicable. "When, in the course of human events, it becomes
necessary for one people to . . ." In one form or another the term
"necessity" recurs throughout the document: "the causes which
impel them to separation"; "it is their *duty* to throw off such
government"; "and such is now the *necessity* which *constrains*

them"; "we *must,* therefore, acquiesce in the *necessity."* Clearly, it is not physical necessity that is being spoken of. The "necessity" here is *moral* necessity—necessity in the order of freedom and obligation.

There had been a "course of human events," eventuating in its *becoming "necessary* for . . ." The point of necessity was reached after stages of argument. The subject of the argument was blandly enough stated by Royal Governor Francis Bernard in November 1765: "It is my opinion that all the political evils in America arise from the want of ascertaining the relations between Great Britain and the American colonies."

In 1768, Benjamin Franklin, not an avid theorist, wrote:

> The more I have thought and read on the subject, the more I find myself confirmed in opinion, that no middle ground can be well maintained, I mean not clearly with intelligible arguments. Something might be made of either of the extremes: that Parliament has a power to make *all laws* for us or a power to make *no laws* for us; and I think the arguments for the latter more numerous and weighty, than those for the former. Supposing that doctrine established, the colonies would then be so many separate states, only subject to the same King, as England and Scotland were before the union.

James Wilson, America's most learned and thoughtful lawyer, firmly argued for what Franklin had called the "more weighty" position in his *Considerations on the Nature and Extent of the Legislative Authority of the British Parliament,* written in 1770, though not published until 1774. In a speech before the Massachusetts Assembly on March 2, 1773, Royal Governor Thomas Hutchinson said, "I know of no line that can be drawn between the supreme authority of Parliament and the total independence of the colonies." Jefferson, in his *A Summary View of the Rights of British America* (1774), agreed with him that "no line could be drawn," found ludicrous the continued reaffirmation of the Declaratory Act that had proclaimed the "supreme authority of the British Parliament," and clearly enough implied that allegiance to the person of the King, to which Franklin had referred, was something voluntary—and revocable.

This had been a constitutional argument, intended by the American leaders to justify their resistance to a whole series of measures, and to disclose those measures as involving constitutional usurpations by the British Parliament, whose authority they came to deny totally. It also cited severe abuses of his prerogatives by the King, to whom they had freely given an allegiance that they could, in right, freely revoke. In the course of the argument, the Americans had conceived and proffered to the British the idea of the Commonwealth that the British belatedly came to in the twentieth century. However, the King closed the argument by ignoring their argued petitions for a redress of grievances, as well as by the military moves he made after declaring the Americans in a state of rebellion. Beyond question, it was only after a fervent effort at genuine argument, and because the argument was closed, that the point of necessity was reached.

The middle section of the Declaration's first complex sentence implicitly contains, as Carl Becker has stated, an important syllogism. The argument can be stated as follows:

Any people, coming, in the course of human events, into historical existence as such, is entitled, by the laws of nature and of nature's God, to assume, among the powers of the earth, a separate and equal station.

The Americans are now a people.

They are, therefore, entitled to such a station.

The mediating term of that momentous syllogism is the term "a people." This term has a complex past throughout Western history. Its applicability has sometimes seemed questionable, as in the cases of the Czechs, Slovaks, Slovenes, Croats, and other such ethnic groups. In recent times, we have seen many "new nations" petition for separate and equal station in the United Nations General Assembly, as if that many distinct "peoples" had suddenly emerged from previously undifferentiated aggregates of humanity.

These examples suggest that claims to the status of "peoplehood" involve such things as a common language, a shared historical experience, and durable cultural traditions. Unquestionably, criteria of this kind are to be found in the American case. However, the definition involved in the Declaration is primarily a sociopolitical and juridical definition, not a historical or cultural one.

Simplified, such a definition might read as follows: A people is a multitude of persons united in the intention of cooperatively pursuing a good human life for all, and large enough and varied enough in its resources to be competent in that associative pursuit.

In the Western tradition, a similar and enduring definition was proposed by Scipio in Cicero's *De Republica:* "A people is not any collection of human beings brought together in any sort of way, but an assemblage of people in large numbers associated in an agreement with respect to justice and a partnership for the common good. [Res publica, res populi, populus autem non omnis hominum coetus quoquo modo congregatus, sed coetus multitudinis iuris consensu et utilitatis communione sociatus.]"

An association of that kind occurs because man is by nature a social animal, by nature in need of the benefits of a directed, orderly association for his pursuit of well-being. It was a traditional and prerevolutionary American doctrine that a people, in the sense defined, had an inherent right to self-rule, an inherent right "to assume among the powers of the earth, the separate and equal station to which the laws of nature and of nature's God entitle them." When an assemblage of men attains the formality of "peoplehood," they constitute a collective person, capable of having rights. A people's right to self-rule was held to be a natural right, derived from the natural right of every individual person to self-rule, taken together with the natural need, implanted in human nature by nature's God, for association as indispensable to the pursuit of happiness.

The second proposition of the syllogistic argument is this: *The Americans are a people.* Carl Becker says that this minor premise "is not explicitly stated in the Declaration." However, it is surely implied, since Jefferson wrote: "When . . . it becomes necessary for *one people* to dissolve the political bands which have connected them with *another* [people]. . . ." Even while there were political bands that tied them together, the Americans were one people, the British another. Jefferson's first draft had read: "becomes necessary for *a people* to advance from the subordination in which they have hitherto remained." In that original wording, corrected probably because the term "subordination" was judged inaccurate, the Americans are spoken of as "a people."

Thomas Hutchinson, the much disliked Royal Governor of Massachusetts, certainly had no doubt that Jefferson intended to be referring to the existence of "a people." After he had returned to England, the former governor, now a self-exiled Loyalist, wrote *Strictures upon the Declaration of the Congress at Philadelphia.* His first stricture read as follows: "They begin with a false hypothesis, that the Colonies are one distinct people, and the kingdom another, connected by political bands. The colonies, politically considered, never were a distinct people from the kingdom. There never has been but one political band and that was just the same before the first colonists emigrated as it has been ever since—the Supreme Legislative Authority, which hath essential right, and is indisputably bound to keep all parts of the Empire entire." It was very late in the day for one more affirmation of the Supreme Parliamentary Authority. However, Hutchinson's denial that "the Colonies are one distinct people, and the kingdom another" reveals his understanding of what Jefferson certainly intended to be affirming.

Hutchinson's reference to "the emigration of the first colonists" also showed his acquaintance with a tract Jefferson had written just two years before—*A Summary View of the Rights of British America* (1774). Jefferson there suggested that the King be reminded

> . . . that our ancestors, before their emigration to America, were the free inhabitants of the British dominions in Europe, and possessed a right, which nature has given to all men, of departing from the country in which chance, not choice has placed them; of going in quest of new habitations, and of there establishing new societies, under such laws and regulations as to them seem most likely to promote public happiness.

Such a position, as Jefferson certainly knew, controverted Blackstone's express provision that no English subject could throw off his natural born allegiance. Jefferson was content to cite the great myth about the Saxon origins of Britain, and to state that "no circumstance has occurred to distinguish materially the British from the Saxon emigration."

As consequences of his view about the meaning of migration, Jefferson proffered these further major opinions in his *Summary View:* that these "new societies" had a right to self-rule; that the British Parliament never had any authority over them; that their adoption of the British common law was something voluntary; that their acts of allegiance to the King were voluntary and, as such, revocable.

Beyond the issues about the juridical meaning of the initial migration, there is a further question, a question that was to persist in a complex and fateful way for a hundred years—the question of "the Union." There were *thirteen* "new societies." Jefferson's argument from the natural right of emigration would apply to each of the thirteen, taken separately. Had these thirteen become "a people," *one* society? An affirmative answer is implicit in our taking July 4, 1776, as the birth date of a new nation. However, that memorial action assumes something to be true; it does not establish its truth.

The answer to the question doubtless must appeal to the çourse of human events in America from 1607 to 1763, and must rely on historical hypotheses about the seedtime and the gestation period.

In the short critical period from 1763 to 1776, the patriots often and eloquently adverted to their "ancestors," proclaiming that a spirit of liberty was a common thread in their great settlement, and that they shared a memory of the difficulty of settling a new land. Clinton Rossiter has presented two texts that illustrate the appeal to ancestors, the first from John Adams, the second from the Reverend William Smith, first Provost of the University of Pennsylvania:

Let us recollect and impress upon our souls the views and ends of our own more immediate forefathers, in exchanging their native country for a dreary, inhospitable wilderness. Let us examine into the nature of that power, and the cruelty of that oppression, which drove them from their homes. Recollect their amazing fortitude, their bitter sufferings,—the hunger, the nakedness, the cold, which they patiently endured,—the severe labors of clearing their grounds, building their houses, raising their provisions, amidst dangers from wild beasts and savage men, before they had time or money or materials for commerce. Recollect the civil and religious principles and hopes and expectations which constantly supported and carried them through all hardships with patience and resignation. Let us recollect it was liberty, the hope of liberty for themselves and us and ours, which conquered all discouragements, dangers, and trials.

Look back, therefore, with reverence look back to the time of ancient virtue and renown. Look back to the mighty purposes which your fathers had in view, when they traversed a vast ocean, and planted this land. Recall to your minds their labors, their toils, their perseverence, and let their divine spirit animate you in all your actions.

The patriots also counted on something else that had been their common heritage: their very considerable common experience of local self-government, which had not, before 1763, been seriously hampered by the presence of royal governors and ministers. In addition, they were aware of and increasingly used a common stock of basic political ideas.

After the strongest case is made for the developing unitive tendencies from 1607 to 1765, there is no disagreement that the decisive unifying events came in the period of resistance. In that period, there were, first, astonishingly quick collective responses of outrage to local British offenses and, then, collective actions of protest. More important, a colonies-wide community of discourse came into being, involving an extraordinary use of all kinds of communications in the press, leading to all kinds of gatherings that the British governors called "unwarrantable assemblies." As early as 1765, John Adams had noted the extent and intensity of the colonial response, which was to quicken sharply in the decade thereafter:

> The people, even to the lowest ranks, have become more attentive to their liberties, more inquisitive about them, and more determined to defend them, than they were ever before known or had occasion to be; innumerable have been the monuments of wit, humor, sense, learning, spirit, patriotism, and heroism, erected in the several colonies and provinces, in the course of this year. Our presses have groaned, our pulpits have thundered, our legislatures have resolved, our towns have voted, the crown officers have every where trembled, and all their little tools and creatures, been afraid to speak and ashamed to be seen.

Committees of correspondence grew up, first within one colony and then, very quickly, between colonies. From such committees of correspondence, and from the colonial assemblies, there issued the calls to the first and second Continental Congresses. The very existence of those Continental Congresses (the adjective was boldly prophetic) amounted to an initial affirmation that the Americans had become *one* people. The resort to arms in resistance occurred after such an all-colony-wide Congress. The Resolution of Independence, declared on July 2, 1776, came from such a Congress. The final confirmation came two days later in the Declaration of Independence, with the statement of the American "case" to "the tribunal of the world."

Definitive decisions about the constitutional and juridical structure of the new nation would have to wait until after the revolutionary war. But the Americans had found and proclaimed their identity as "a people." They had done so after skillful actions of resistance to oppression, but, even more so, after sustained, impassioned, widespread argument in support of those actions. It was the experience of that argument that led to the wholly unprecedented document of July 4. Never before had colonists, rebelling from an imperial power, judged that "a decent respect to the opinions of mankind requires that they should declare the causes which impel them to the separation."

Before proceeding to the factual indictment of the King, and implicitly of Parliament, in support of the judgment that the Americans had been subjected to intolerable injustices, Jefferson first indicates, in the second paragraph of the Declaration, the fundamental principles—the political philosophy—underlying such a judgment.

We hold these truths . . .

This economical, forthright, double-edged assertion contains two important propositions: On the one hand, it asserts that there *are* truths regulative of deliberation and decision in a crisis of human events, and, on the other hand, it asserts that *we*—the people—*affirm* them.

It is often said that such boldness of statement was characteristic of the optimistic rationalism of the eighteenth-century Enlightenment. That is misleading. From the beginning, and increasingly throughout the tradition of the West, it was thought that truths about the nature of man, about natural rights, and about the purpose of government could be discovered and affirmed—indeed, must be if the association of men in political communities or civil societies was to be both reasonable and just.

. . . to be self-evident, . . .

This, too, has been deemed overrationalistic, naïve, or an extravagant rhetorical flourish. However, we have no reason to suppose Jefferson ignorant of the traditional technical meaning of "self-evident" in the sciences of logic and mathematics. He was acquainted with the axioms of Euclid's geometry, which, as distinguished from the theorems, are affirmable without demonstration and, therefore, are self-evident. This conception of the axiomatic or self-evident differs from the notion that the self-evident is simply the obvious. Many statements may be accepted by many persons as obvious that, upon examination, are not in the strict logical sense self-evident.

In that strict logical sense, a proposition is self-evident only if its truth cannot be demonstrated and only if its opposite is inconceivable. What makes it true in this special way? Consider, for example, one of Euclid's axioms—that the whole is greater than the part. Our understanding of the two principal terms in this proposition—*whole* and *part*—is such that we immediately understand them to be related in a certain way, the one greater than the other, and we cannot conceive them to be related in the opposite way—the whole less than the part. If we could, the proposition would not be logically self-evident, nor would it be if we could somehow prove that whole and part must be related in this way by a process of reasoning in which we introduced other terms that enabled us to establish the stated relationship between whole and part.

That no other terms can be introduced as mediators between whole and part makes our understanding of their relationship immediate (that is, without mediators), and that immediacy is essential to a proposition's being self-evident—known to be true from its own terms without appeal to any others. This is a logical, not a psychological, criterion, since the truth which can be immediately known in this way may not be obvious to someone who has not grasped the meaning of its terms. The meanings of the terms in some self-evident propositions may require prolonged reflection before they are adequately comprehended. The proposition here declared a self-evident truth—that all men are equal—is certainly less obvious than the axiom concerning the relation between a whole and its parts.

Two further observations are germane at this point. First, the statement about human equality held to be a self-evident truth is declarative or descriptive, not imperative or prescriptive. It is a statement of fact, not an injunction to action. Even if it is correct to say that each of us should treat his fellow men as equal, or that all men ought to be so treated, it is not self-evidently so; nor would it be possible to defend or support the soundness of the injunction if there were, as a matter of fact, no respect in which it is true that all men are equal.

Second, it must be acknowledged that the immediately following clauses in the Declaration state truths that are not self-evident in the strict logical sense. That men are endowed with certain inalienable rights, that these include the rights to life, liberty, and the pursuit of happiness, that governments derive their just powers from the consent of the governed—these propositions can be staunchly defended as true, but precisely because they need to be and can be defended by arguments, they are not self-evident. With regard to this logical blemish, some later words of Alexander Hamilton are germane. Hamilton opens *Federalist* #31 with a short disquisition on "primary truths or first principles." After citing several "maxims in geometry," such as "the whole is greater than its part," and also "maxims in ethics and politics," such as "the means ought to be proportioned to the end," Hamilton makes the following statement:

> And there are other truths in the two latter sciences which, if they cannot pretend to rank in the class of axioms, are yet such direct inferences from them . . . that they challenge the assent of a sound and unbiased mind, with a degree of force and conviction almost equally irresistible.

In Jefferson's mind, the propositions that follow "all men are created equal" certainly had that kind of force.

> . . . that *all men are* (created) *equal;* . . .

Ignoring for the moment the presence of the term "created," the questions to be answered in an effort to construe this proposition as a self-evident truth concern the meaning of its two principal terms —"men" and "equal."

It is not necessary to assume that the signers of the Declaration had a common verbal formula to express their understanding of what was meant by the term "man." However, there is ample evidence that their concept of human nature, expressed in one or another form of words, reflected the traditional teaching that man is a person, not a thing—a rational being with free choice, aspiring to the fulfillment of his natural propensities or capacities and, because he is free, morally responsible for what he does or does not do to achieve that goal. Because the traditional doctrine also maintained that man is not only a rational, but also a social and political, animal, the signers would also have understood that each individual depends upon his association with other human beings for an effective pursuit of that goal—sometimes called happiness, sometimes a good human life, and sometimes self-realization or self-perfection.

What was meant by the term "equal" in the Declaration's statement that "all men are equal"? Since anyone can easily find in experience so many different respects in which individual men are clearly not equal, a special meaning must be assigned to this term in the statement about *all* men if the proposition is to be interpreted in a way that makes it self-evidently true. The only meaning which serves that purpose is the equality of all men *as men*—their sameness as human beings, a sameness which underlies their individual differences in all other respects. Though one human being may be more or less than another in every other respect, none is more or less human in consequence of that; and so they are equal as human beings even though they may be unequal, one with another, in every other respect.

This understanding of the equality of men as men also involves conceiving human beings as equal in their possession of the dignity which attaches to being human, a dignity not possessed by other things. It involves conceiving them as sharing in what is common to all members of the human species—the powers or properties that distinguish men from other animals, together with the natural aspirations rooted in their common nature, such as the aspirations for happiness.

If this is a correct interpretation of the self-evidence of the truth that all men are equal, it reflects a conviction on the part of the signers concerning the reality of the common human nature in which all men participate as members of the same species. They did not use the words "man" and "human" merely as verbal tags for an arbitrary grouping in some scheme of classification adopted for purely practical reasons.

Understood in this way, the equality of human beings as all possessing the same dignity has profound consequences. It imposes obligations of mutual respect on those who enter into association with one another in order to make good human lives for themselves.

Acknowledging implicitly that all men may not in fact be treated as equal, it implies that all should be so treated.

... that all men are *created* equal; ...

The proposition in the Declaration is not "all men are equal," but rather "all men are created equal."

It should not be supposed that Jefferson regarded the theological doctrine of creation as self-evident. That God exists, that God created the universe and all things in it, that man is a creature of God—these are articles of religious faith; or, if their truth can be known by reason, such knowledge would result from long and difficult lines of reasoning in natural theology. In any case, they are not self-evident. Jefferson's reference to creation must be construed as an implicit acknowledgment of the prevailing religious beliefs or philosophical convictions of his day. The clause could have been expanded to make that acknowledgment explicit and also separate from the affirmation of a self-evident truth: "All men, their nature having been created by God, are equal in their common nature as human beings."

In its traditional formulation, the theory of natural law, with which the doctrine of natural rights is associated, rested on a theological foundation. The laws of nature were the laws of nature's God. To regard them in this way gave them authority and sanctions they would not otherwise have. So, too, if human nature is created by God, then the natural moral law and the natural rights, which can be discovered by reflection on the natural propensities and natural needs of human beings, have a transcendental origin. Nevertheless, the discovery of the natural moral law, or of the rights inherently possessed by all men because of their common human nature, in no way depends on the belief that God is the creator of human nature and thus the ultimate source of natural law. Nor does disbelief in God as creator alter the consequences that flow from the affirmation that men are equal as men. In a famous passage in his Prolegomena to *On the Law of War and Peace,* which some of the founding fathers knew, Grotius, a believing Protestant, had written that the natural laws of right and wrong would still have great weight, "even if we were to grant, what we cannot grant without wickedness, that there is no God, or that he bestows no regard on human affairs."

In his compressed five words, Jefferson recorded the prevailing American view that human equality and natural rights enjoyed both divine sanction and the sanction of right reason.

. . . that they are endowed by their Creator . . .

The reference to a transcendental source is here repeated. The endowment, however, refers to attributes of the nature created, attributes that derive from the natural equality of men. In his first draft Jefferson had made that point quite explicit, writing "from that equal creation they derive rights inherent and inalienable." The endowment, then, consisted of natural rights—rights inherent in nature. Though an appeal to right reason might suffice for the recognition of such rights, here as before the reference to the Creator gave them an additional and higher sanction, according to the view prevalent at the time. Attempts to violate such rights or to render them void would be an offense against the Creator, whose intention was declared in the nature created.

. . . with certain unalienable rights; . . .

The negative word in this clause gives a clue to the character of the rights conceived as man's natural endowment. The civil or legal rights that the state confers on its citizens or subjects by positive enactment or constitutional provision, it can revoke or nullify. They are alienable. To say that certain rights are inalienable is to say their possession by men does not depend upon legislation of any kind. They are inalienable because they are inherent in the nature of man. They belong to human beings in virtue of their being human. They have moral force and impose moral obligations even when they lack legal force and lack legal sanctions. They can, therefore, be called "moral rights" or "human rights" as well as "natural rights." Though these denominations are not identical in their connotation, all three refer to rights that are not dependent for their existence upon positive law or political institutions.

While the existence of such rights does not depend upon the constitution or the laws of the state, the enforcement of them does. A particular state may or may not give constitutional or legal recognition to the rights here declared to be inalienable; and accordingly, states may be judged on moral grounds or principles of justice in terms of their respect or disrespect for these moral, human, or natural rights.

As already noted, these rights impose moral obligations: They are rights that should be respected by everyone under all circumstances. Their inalienability, however, does not preclude limitations upon the exercise of these rights, limitations that may be justified under certain circumstances. An individual may forfeit by misconduct his exercise of rights that are inherent in him, but he cannot abnegate his possession of them. They cannot be given away by him any more than they can be taken away from him by others.

The fact that the attribution to men of certain inalienable rights follows directly upon the affirmation that all men are equal by nature as well as by divine creation, has profound significance. If the rights in question are inherent in human nature, and if the equality of men is rooted in the sameness of the specific nature in which all men participate, then these human or moral rights are equally possessed by all. Some men do not have more claim and others less claim to the entitlement of these rights. Whatever any human being is entitled to by virtue of his human rights, all other human beings are equally entitled to.

> . . . that *among these* are life, liberty, and the pursuit of happiness.

The phrase "among these" plainly implies that there are other natural, human, or moral rights in addition to the three mentioned. Questions arise, therefore, concerning what these other rights might be and how they stand in relation to the rights specifically mentioned, as well as why, of all the rights that might have been mentioned, only these three were named in the Declaration.

For the question about the range and variety of inherent and inalienable rights, we are provided with an impressively detailed answer in the Universal Declaration of Human Rights adopted by the United Nations. The fact that the United Nations, because it lacks the coercive force of a sovereign government, cannot enact legislation "to secure these rights" on a worldwide basis does not alter the significance of the declaration itself, or diminish the importance of the fact that its signatories were representatives of all the peoples of the world.[1]

[1] See Appendix for the enumeration of rights in the Universal Declaration of Human Rights.

The declaration of human or natural rights by the United Nations enumerates rights that probably would not have been included in a list drawn up in the eighteenth century that might then have been thought comprehensive. Though such a list might have been enlarged in the nineteenth century, it still would have fallen short of the enumeration made in our own time. This historical fact requires us to consider how these rights are discovered, and why rights that are supposedly natural and human should be only progressively discovered in the course of time. What obstacles delayed their discovery? Why were they not always known?

Such questions themselves have undergone historical changes. The whole doctrine of natural law and natural rights was discredited in the nineteenth century when it was presented in a distorted version. According to that mistaken view, human nature is an open, well-illuminated book from which, by simple inspection, manuals of natural laws and lists of natural rights can be produced. If that were the case, there could be no explanation of the progressive enlargement of the rights enumerated in succeeding centuries, nor any reason for the delay in discovering certain rights not mentioned at earlier times. An explanation is available, however, on the traditional view of the process by which such rights are discovered. According to that traditional view, the effort to discover the precepts of the natural moral law and the specific rights to which all human beings are naturally entitled is subject to the same conditions of error and delayed progress that prevail in other spheres of knowledge.

Our expanding knowledge of celestial phenomena, for example, has depended at crucial stages of progress upon the invention and use of more and more powerful instruments of observation. What we have learned only recently through improved instrumentation did not come into existence recently. Before we were able to observe and describe them, the phenomena were as they are now. It is not the phenomena that have altered or grown; it is only our knowledge of them. So, too, in the case of natural rights: They have not increased in number in succeeding centuries; rather our knowledge of them has enlarged.

What plays a role analogous to the role played by improved instrumentation in astronomy? One answer that has been given to this difficult question is that, in the course of history, the altered circumstances of social life, including technological advances as well as institutional innovations, have removed emotional obstacles to the exercise of reason needed to discover natural rights. It has also been argued that the conscience of mankind has grown more sensitive in the course of time and under the pressure of events.

Jefferson himself provides us with testimony in support of the view that the recognition of certain rights waits on advances in man's moral consciousness, advances that are not come by easily. He was profoundly uneasy about the flagrant contradiction between the institution of slavery and the equality of men, together with their equal possession of the natural right to liberty. He deplored that "execrable commerce . . . a market where men could be bought and sold." This led him to introduce into his indictment of George III, clumsily and unconvincingly, his abhorrence of chattel slavery as a patent violation of a natural, human right. For reasons of policy quite pragmatic, the Congress struck from the document that part of his draft.

Even if they had no other examples than those of chattel slavery and racial discrimination, the American people can learn, from the birth conditions and the birth document of their country, how startlingly slow the constitutional enactment and legal enforcement of natural rights can be. However, the laggard pace in the development of the conscience of mankind yields an argument against the doctrine of natural rights only on the mistaken view that natural rights can be discovered easily. Further, the pages of history make unmistakably clear that, even when the reason and conscience of mankind do affirm certain rights to be inalienably human, they are not forthwith enacted into law.

Jefferson singled out three rights which he clearly regarded as the most fundamental ones to affirm in the Declaration of Independence.

> . . . that among these are *life, liberty, and the pursuit of happiness.*

Why did Jefferson choose this triad of basic rights? Can it be contended that they are the principal or most fundamental rights to which all others are subordinate as means to the ends they serve? The argument for that contention, severely foreshortened, might run as follows:

An understanding of human nature, derived from reflection on human experience and human history, leads to the recognition of certain obligations that a man must discharge in order to fulfill himself as a man. He ought to strive to preserve his very existence. Being endowed with freedom of choice, he ought to strive to control the course of his life. And in exercising his freedom to choose the direction of his life, he ought to strive to make it a good life; he ought to strive for self-perfection, for the fullest development of his potentialities—for happiness.

To implement the discharge of these obligations, a man must have the right to life, liberty, and the pursuit of happiness: the right to life being his right to security against forces or factors inimical to its preservation; the right to liberty being his right to conditions or circumstances favoring or facilitating the carrying out in action of the choices he makes; and the right to the pursuit of happiness being his right to whatever help organized society can give him in his effort to make a good human life for himself. These rights involve binding claims about what is due each man from his fellow men and about what is due him from organized society and from a government that is instituted to secure such rights.

In further support of the contention that Jefferson's famous triad of inalienable rights are the principal or most fundamental of all human or natural rights, it must be argued that no other rights are on the same level, because all others are rights to the things a man needs in order to preserve his life, exercise his freedom, and pursue happiness. Thus, for example, when at a later time it is declared that a man has a right to a living wage—a right to earn a living for himself—that right can be seen as a specific determination of a man's right to life or self-preservation.

While life, liberty, and happiness are coordinately goods that each human being naturally desires to preserve or promote, happiness alone is the ultimate goal that is desired for its own sake and not as a means to anything beyond itself. Because of this, even the rights to life and liberty can be viewed as auxiliary or instrumental to the pursuit of happiness, for life and liberty are indispensable means thereto. A human being's moral obligation to make a good life for himself not only grounds his right to pursue happiness but also encompasses all other rights—rights to whatever is indispensable to the pursuit of happiness, such as the preservation of life and the protection of liberty, and still other rights subordinate to these.

The temptation to consider Jefferson's selective triad of rights an inspired choice is engendered especially by the act of substitution he performed with regard to the third element in that triad. Jefferson was acquainted with John Locke's formulation of fundamental rights. Locke's triad had been "life, liberty, and property" or "life, liberty, and estates." Persistently in the prerevolutionary literature, Locke's triad had been reiterated and had been regarded as almost canonical. It is, therefore, difficult to believe that Jefferson's substitution of "the pursuit of happiness" for "property" or "estates" was not deliberate.

Not only did he introduce this striking revision of Locke's phrasing, but he also departed even further from the statement made by his close friend and fellow Virginian George Mason. Less than a month before July 4, 1776, the Virginia Constitutional Convention had adopted a Declaration of Rights drafted by Mason. Section 1 of that Declaration read as follows:

> That all men are by nature equally free and independent and have certain inherent rights, of which, when they enter into a state of society, they cannot, by any compact, deprive or divest their posterity; namely, *the enjoyment of life and liberty, with the means of acquiring and possessing property, and pursuing and obtaining happiness and safety.*

It is clear that Jefferson picked up the inherent right of pursuing happiness. It is just as clear that he decided against including Mason's phrase "the means of acquiring and possessing property"; not only that, but also, and even more significantly, he deliberately converted Mason's "pursuing and obtaining happiness and safety" into "the pursuit of happiness."

With regard to the revision of Locke and Mason on property, we know that at a later time Jefferson, in discussing the French Bill of Rights with his friend Lafayette, counseled him against the inclusion of the right to property. There is no reason to think that Jefferson meant to deny that there was a right to property. If it were stated with suitable generality, open to varying determinations by positive laws under changing economic circumstances, he would probably have considered that right a natural right. Even so, he would not have regarded it as being on the same fundamental level as the rights to life, liberty, and the pursuit of happiness. The substitution of that third right for the right of property gave Jefferson's declaration of rights a universality and scope that could not otherwise have been achieved; for it was open to and could cover whatever insights about enabling means for the pursuit of happiness that societies and governments might subsequently discover in the ongoing historical effort to provide human beings with the conditions they need for their well-being and welfare. The possession of property, or its economic equivalents, is certainly only one of such conditions.

The significance of Jefferson's substitution of the pursuit of happiness for property is enhanced by his alteration of Mason's phrasing of this matter. Where Mason spoke of "pursuing *and obtaining* happiness *and safety,*" Jefferson dropped the words "obtaining" and "safety." Reference to safety as something to be paired with or coordinate with happiness weakened the conception of happiness as life's ultimate objective—the goal to be striven for. If the word "safety" meant security of life and limb, it was already covered by the right to life and so should not be mentioned again, certainly not as coordinate with the pursuit of happiness, to which such security may be an indispensable means, but only a means.

In addition, one can surmise that it was Jefferson's understanding of the traditional meaning of the term "happiness" that led him to formulate the human right with regard to it as the right of pursuing it, but not the right of obtaining it. In the traditional philosophical conception of happiness as a life well lived, or a good life as a whole, the achievement of happiness depended on the individual's possession of certain virtues that are entirely within his own power to acquire. If he fails to acquire them, he alone is to blame. No organized society or instituted government can confer moral virtue upon him or make him a man of good moral character; and so, the attainment of happiness being dependent on a man's interior moral disposition, no society or government could ever secure an individual's right to obtain or achieve happiness. A right that cannot be secured by any devisable institutional means is void of political meaning. What organized societies and instituted governments can do is to provide human beings with the external conditions indispensable to the *pursuit* of happiness, facilitating but not ensuring its attainment. The right to pursue happiness is, therefore, a right to these indispensable external conditions—conditions specified by all the other rights which are subordinate to the right of pursuing happiness.

Jefferson's grasp of the traditional conception of happiness impelled him to correct Mason's error in supposing that governments can secure the right to "obtain" happiness. That supposition fails to recognize the limitations of government and betrays a misunderstanding of the purely personal factors involved in the pursuit of happiness. However, stress on these personal factors may lead to another error that must be guarded against for an understanding of the full truth of Jefferson's fundamental insight concerning the pursuit of happiness as the most fundamental of all human rights.

While each individual must be free to pursue happiness in his own way, given the individuality of his own personal endowments and the special circumstances of his own life, the goal he is striving to achieve—the good human life he is trying to make for himself—is not distinctly individual but humanly common. The happy or good life is essentially the same for all human beings; it is a fulfillment of the same specifically human potentialities or propensities; it is a satisfaction of the same needs inherent in human nature. Whatever things are really good for any human being are really good for all other human beings; and so if happiness consists in a life enriched by all the things that are really good for a man, happiness is the same for all men.

If the contrary view is held, that happiness consists in what each individual wants for himself, and differs according to individual desires or inclinations, then no government could possibly secure for all their right to its pursuit, since the wants or desires of one individual so often come into conflict with those of another. What we must suppose Jefferson to have understood is that unless the pursuit of happiness is cooperative rather than competitive, it would be beyond the power of government to secure this right for all. To be a goal that can be pursued by all without one individual interfering with or impeding another, happiness or the good life must consist in common, not individual, goods—goods that are the same for all and can be participated in by all.

Having drawn from the natural equality of men their equal possession of fundamental natural rights, the Declaration goes on to the role of the government in relation to those rights.

> That, to secure these rights, governments are instituted among men, . . .

The statement that governments are instituted among men to secure these rights should not be read as a statement of historical

fact. Jefferson certainly knew from political history that governments come into being in a variety of ways and for a variety of
purposes. Not all are instituted, for some are imposed by force, and
even of those which are instituted not all are instituted to secure the
rights of man for all men.

Jefferson's choice of the word "instituted" is hardly accidental.
He certainly understood that only governments that are instituted
rather than imposed by force would be governments that might
serve the purpose of securing human rights. Only such governments,
voluntarily adopted or, as he goes on to say, established by "the
consent of the governed," would be concerned with protecting the
rights of the governed as opposed to serving the self-interest of
those governing by imposed force. The line thus drawn between
governments imposed and governments instituted divides governments by might from governments by right.

The word "just," which makes its appearance in the next clause,
reflects back upon what is here being said. Not all governments are
just, either in the way they hold power or in the way they exercise
it. Their possession of power is just only to the extent that the
powers they have are legitimate or authorized because they derive
from the consent of the people who have voluntarily adopted the
constitution or framework of a government that is instituted by
them. Possessing legitimate or authorized power, a government
exercises such power justly only to the extent that it respects the
inherent and inalienable rights of man and attempts to secure them,
not just for some men, but for all.

Though the great compression under which he is writing may at
first conceal or obscure his meaning, Jefferson certainly has these
criteria of justice in mind in his statement about the origin and
purpose of government. He is thinking normatively, not descriptively or historically. If what he has in mind were to be stated normatively rather than descriptively, the statement would read as
follows: Governments *should be* instituted among men and they
should be instituted to serve the purpose that governments *ought*
to serve, namely, to secure these rights—the inalienable rights previously named as well as other rights not specifically mentioned.

Jefferson's compact statement of the purpose a government must
serve in order to be just echoes an equally compact statement cur-
rent in the Middle Ages, which defined the purpose of government
in the following formula: servitium propter jura, non potestas

praeter jura (service to and for the sake of rights, not a power exercised beyond or outside of rights). Any more elaborate formulation of the end to be served by a just government should be interpretable as an amplifying specification of the Declaration's succinct statement.

What appears to be an alternative formulation of the purpose of government is given in the Preamble to the Constitution, in which the elements of the common good are articulated as the several distinct objectives of government. Included among them are such things as union, civil peace or domestic tranquility, national security, and the general welfare. Each of these is an aspect of the good that is common to all members of the community, something in which they all share; but so, too, are the inalienable rights of man elements in the common good, for they are rights common to all members of the community, rights equally possessed by all. These alternative statements about the purpose of government—the one in the Declaration and the one in the Preamble—must, therefore, be read as supplementary rather than as conflicting. In one respect, however, the statement in the Declaration is more philosophical, in that it appeals to the criteria of justice by which legitimate or constitutional governments are to be distinguished from illegitimate or despotic regimes, and by which one legitimate government can be judged to be more or less just than another.

Attention must be paid to the critical verb "to secure" in the Declaration's statement of the purpose of government. Just governments are not instituted to endow men with these rights, or to confer these rights upon them, for human beings already possess these rights by virtue of their being human. The right interpretation can be drawn from the etymology of the term "secure"—from the grave, complex beauty of the Latin word *cura.* Just governments are instituted among men in order to assure them they can be *without care,* without anxiety or apprehension, about the opportunity to exercise within society rights that are naturally theirs. These rights are safeguarded by a government that is just in the exercise of its powers.

> . . . deriving their just powers from the consent of
> the governed; . . .

The purpose for which just governments are instituted having been stated, a related but different question arises: What is the source of the authority for the powers such governments will exercise? The preceding discussion has already anticipated the answer to be given—but only in part. A fuller statement of the answer must expatiate on a basic principle in the tradition of Western constitutionalism. Jefferson appealed to that principle and was aware of the dispute concerning the sources of authority that had permeated Western political and juridical history.

The powers of a government are just and legitimate only if they are authorized powers, that is, if they derive their authority from the consent of the governed, for they can gain authority in no other way. The reason is the people's right to self-rule; they inherently possess the authority to govern themselves. If, in doing so, they erect or institute an apparatus of government in the form of public offices each exercising certain administrative powers (legislative, judicial, or executive), they confer legitimacy upon these powers by transmitting or imparting to them the authority that ultimately and permanently resides in the people.

This principle of transmitted authority through consent had been variously stated in the tradition of political thought with which Jefferson was acquainted. A well-known and recurrently expressed medieval maxim read: Quod omnes tangit, ab omnibus approbetur (whatever touches all must be approved by all). Sir John Fortescue, Chief Justice of the King's Bench under Henry VI and, along with Bracton, one of the most eminent jurists in England's early constitutional history, appealed to the principle of consent in distinguishing between an absolute and a constitutional monarch. The latter, he wrote, "may not rule his people by other laws than such as they assent to. And therefore he may set upon them no impositions without their consent."

The principle of consent appeared later in the famous debate held in 1647 within the General Council of Oliver Cromwell's army, in the short period between the first and second civil wars. Where Fortescue and other medieval jurists employed the principle of consent to define the limitations on the law-making power of a constitutional monarch, in the debate within Cromwell's army the consent of the governed was used to envision the ideal of a constitutional democracy. The debate occurred in the context of proposals for the extension of the suffrage to the nonpropertied classes in the population. These proposals were put forward in a draft constitution entitled "An Agreement of the People," sponsored by the so-called

Levellers who reflected the opinions of the rank and file in Cromwell's regiments. The Levellers were later suppressed by Cromwell, who, with his son-in-law Colonel Henry Ireton, defended the privileged position of the propertied classes. Though they lost at the time, the Levellers won the argument in subsequent history. The statements they made in the course of the debate were quoted again and again at critical moments in the development of modern democratic theory.

The most striking of these statements was the one made by Major William Rainborough, a leader of the Levellers:

> For really I think that the poorest he that is in England hath a life to live, as the greatest he; and therefore truly, sir, I think it is clear that every man that is to live under a government ought first by his own *consent* to put himself under that government; and I do think that the poorest man in England is not at all bound in a strict sense to that government that he hath not had a voice to put himself under.

The transition in thought here from every man's equal right to pursue happiness (equality in having "a life to live") to every man's right to be governed only with his consent is as swift as it is in the succession of Jefferson's clauses in the Declaration of Independence. Major Rainborough's views are somewhat more expansively expressed in a later statement by a fellow Leveller, Sir John Wildman, who spoke as follows:

> We are now engaged for our freedom. That is the end of parliaments: not to constitute what is already [established, but to act] according to the just rules of government. Every person in England hath as clear a right to elect his representative as the greatest person in England. I conceive that is the undeniable maxim of government: that all government is in the free consent of the people. If [so], then upon that account there is no person that is under a just government, or hath justly his own, unless he by his own free consent be put under that government. This he cannot be unless he be consenting to it, and therefore, according to this maxim, there is never a person in England [but ought to have a voice in elections]. If [this], as that gentleman says, be true, there are no laws that in this strictness and rigor of justice [any man is bound to], that are not made by those . . . he doth consent to. And therefore I should humbly move, that if the question be stated—

which would soonest bring things to an issue—it might rather be thus: *Whether any person can justly be bound by law, who doth not give his consent that such persons shall make laws for him?*

The Levellers, it should be noted, used the principle of consent to argue for universal manhood suffrage—a franchise not restricted by property qualifications. They were greatly in advance of their time, for the struggle to extend the franchise to all, and to secure for all the right to participate in self-government, did not gain ground, either in England or in the United States, until the middle of the nineteenth century and, with respect to the female half of the population, not until the twentieth. In Jefferson's day, the consent of the governed would certainly not have been interpreted as the consent of the whole population that was subject to government, but rather as the consent of those then regarded as qualified to participate in self-government. The line that separated those presumed to be competent to exercise a voice in the adoption or constitution of the framework of government from those who must passively submit to its authority and power would also divide the enfranchised citizens of the republic from its disfranchised subjects —women, blacks, the unpropertied. However, if we read Jefferson's appeal to the principle of consent in the immediate context of his affirmation of every man's natural right to liberty—a liberty that certainly includes political liberty, the freedom of the citizen as a participant in the self-government of a free people—then the principle of consent cries out for universal suffrage.

The principle is of such importance to the emergence and defense of constitutional democracy that it is worth more attention. The state of the argument about it and about its relation to the doctrine of human equality and the right to liberty, during the revolutionary period, can be discerned in a brief passage from Jonathan Boucher's *A View of the Causes and Consequences of the American Revolution.* This pamphlet was written in England after Boucher had fled the American colonies in 1775, in fear of his life because of the ire he aroused by his defense of the conservative Loyalist position. In the twelfth discourse of that book, Boucher undertook to argue against a sermon delivered by the Reverend Mr. Duché in Philadelphia in 1775, a sermon on a text from Galatians: "Stand fast, therefore, in the liberty wherewith Christ hath made us free." Boucher responded as follows:

[His premise], therefore, that "the common good is matter of common feeling," being false, the consequence drawn from it, viz., that government was instituted by "common consent," is of course equally false.

This popular notion that government was originally formed by the consent or by a compact of the people rests on, and is supported by, another similar notion, not less popular nor better founded. This other notion is that the whole human race is born equal; and that no man is naturally inferior or, in any respect, subjected to another; and that he can be made subject to another only by his own consent. The position is equally ill-founded and false both in its premises and conclusions.

This passage can be taken as negative testimony to the remarkable impetus that Jefferson gave to the nascent idea of democracy by placing the principle of consent in the context of an affirmation of human equality and of the right to liberty. Boucher, in a sermon delivered in Virginia before he left this country, had also argued for the divine right of kings, viewing the monarch as the vicegerent of God, drawing his authority immediately from the deity he represented on earth. Jefferson, in sharp contrast, not only echoed the seventeenth-century Levellers in his view that the authority or legitimacy of government rested on the consent of the governed, but also harked back to the medieval doctrine stated by Thomas Aquinas, that the king, or any other ruling body, acts as vicegerent for and draws authority from the people, in whom God has vested that authority—the authority to govern themselves, either directly or through the instrumentality of vicegerents or representatives.

Other theories of political authority, such as the doctrine that it belongs to rulers by prescriptive possession based on a right they have by long-standing custom (jure consuetudinario), as well as the theory that it is theirs by right of divine assignment directly to them, bypassed the people entirely. Only the doctrine of consent enthroned the people as the fountainhead of authority; it is from the people as sovereign that authority is transmitted to whoever holds public office as their vicegerents or representatives.

This conception of the transmission of authority had a classical origin in ancient Roman history. Because it succeeded the Roman Republic, the Empire, when it first came into being, saw fit to pay lip service to the republican principle of the consent of the governed. It did so by means of a juridical fiction, first formulated by

Ulpian and later canonized by Justinian in his codification of
Roman law. The formula ran as follows:

> Quod principi placuit, legis habet vigorem, cum lege regia, quae
> de imperio eius lata est, populus ei et in eum omne suum im-
> perium et potestatem concessit.

> Whatever pleases the emperor has the force of law, since by the
> royal law, which has been laid down concerning his authority, the
> people conceded to him and into his hands all its authority and
> power.

In this great fictional event, the transfer of authority from the
people to the Emperor was presented as a total and irrevocable
transmission. The transition from the Republic to the Empire was
pictured as a point of no return, the people pictured as having com-
pletely abdicated their sovereignty. In sharp contrast, the later
Western theory of republican or constitutional government regarded
the transmission of authority from the people to their representatives as neither total nor final and irrevocable: not total, because
limitations were to be placed on the powers vested in public offices
by a constitution; not final or irrevocable, because provisions were
to be made to keep officeholders accountable to the citizens they
represented. Officials were to be judged by the people with regard
to their exercise of the just—or authorized—powers derived from
the consent of the governed.

> . . . that, whenever any form of government becomes
> destructive of these ends, it is the right of the people
> to alter or to abolish it, . . .

A government, instituted by the people and deriving its just
powers from their consent, would continue and might endure so
long as it earns that consent. But precisely because the consensual
transmission of authority was not final or irrevocable, the people
retain, as part of their original and standing right to self-rule, the
right to alter and abolish a government that departs from or trans-
gresses the ends for which a form of government had been instituted
in the first place. This right to alter or abolish is simply the other
face of the right to erect or constitute a framework of government
for the effective exercise of self-rule.

So long as a people does not exercise its right to alter or abolish, it can be construed as giving both the form of government it has constituted and also the administration of that government its continuing consent on the grounds that both have served the ends or the objective assigned—the securing of human rights. However, when, for whatever reason, a form of government fails to serve these ends or its administration subverts them and usurps unauthorized power (power not consented to), then the people have a right to withdraw their consent. This right, often called "the right of revolution," provides the grounds of justification for a change in government, either partial (i.e., alteration) or total (i.e., abolition).

That change, whether partial or total, need not involve insurrectionary violence or open civil war, though, in the usual course of events, it probably would. Civil dissent, or dissent within the boundaries of consent, should be able to bring about legislative reforms or changes in public policy without recourse to violence. But once consent itself has been withdrawn by all or by a preponderant majority, there is little hope for a peaceful resolution of the conflict between a people that wishes to preserve its rights and liberties and those who wish to continue in power—power that has now become sheer might, for it has been deprived of any right or authority because of the withdrawal of consent by the governed. If the arbitrament of war cannot be avoided, the responsibility for it, John Locke had observed, rests on those who have provoked the withdrawal of consent by exceeding the authority conferred on them.

. . . and to institute new government, . . .

The purpose behind the impulse to abolish an existing form of government is not to do away with government itself. Jefferson may have been a minimalist with regard to the extent of government that is desirable, but he was certainly not an anarchist wishing to dispense with government entirely. Rebellion may, indeed, involve a return to the state of war, but it does not aim at a return to the state of nature—in which each man is judge in his own case and can preserve his rights and liberties only by the resort to force, since he is without recourse to laws and tribunals.

A revolution is a change in the form of government. It has two stages: the alteration or abolition of an existing government, and the institution of a reformed or a new government. On the eleventh anniversary of the Declaration of Independence, the poet and diplomat Joel Barlow, addressing the Society of the Cincinnati at Hartford, Connecticut, said:

> Whenever praise is due for the task already performed, it is certain that much remains to be done. The Revolution is but half completed. Independence and government were the two objects contended for, and but one is yet obtained.

It was fitting that in the Declaration of Independence Jefferson, speaking for a people that intended to assume an equal station among the powers of the earth, would assure a candid world that, after independence had been won, the new free people would proceed with all deliberate speed to institute a new government. The Constitution of the United States emerged from the convention for ratification by the people less than three months after Barlow's eleventh anniversary address. The effort had been difficult and the progress deliberate but not unduly prolonged.

. . . laying its foundations on such principles, and organizing its powers in such form, as to them shall seem most likely to effect their safety and happiness.

"Laying its foundations on such principles . . ." There is little doubt that Jefferson intended the word "such" to be retroactive, referring to the fundamental equality of men and their equal possession of natural rights. Such principles, and only these, in Jefferson's mind, could yield the true end of just government—the securing to all men of their human rights.

The point is not of slight importance. Jefferson expected that the same principles that impelled the colonies to declare their independence would also preside over the subsequent institution of a new government and would regulate deliberation about how it should be constituted. He expected continuity on the level of principle and fundamental purpose from the initiating to the consummating moment of the American Revolution. An argument about whether such continuity or conformity was being achieved occurred in what newspapers of the time called "The Grand Convention of 1787." The argument raged throughout the course of the first three administrations, during which Jefferson became increasingly furious as he observed the use that Alexander Hamilton was making of the new constitution to subvert, in Jefferson's phrases, "the spirit of '76" and "the principles declared in 1776."

"And organizing its powers . . ." This is Jefferson's prevision of what remained to be done in the second moment of the Revolution. Though his phrasing is highly compressed, it indicates what is involved in the making of a constitution, which, according to ancient political thought, is an organization of offices with limited powers assigned to each. The constitution to be drafted after independence had been won would be precisely such a charter, setting forth the offices in the several departments of government, relating them to one another in a functional plan of organization, and prescribing the powers they would exercise as well as what powers would be reserved.

"In such form . . ." From the Greeks onward, political philosophy had considered the problem of diverse forms of government and had been concerned with their definition, classification, and evaluation. The most fundamental distinction made in antiquity was that between royal and constitutional government—a government by men, men above all laws, and a government of laws, laws above all men. Constitutional government was one of the major types of government; royal or, as it is sometimes called, absolute or despotic government another. But not all constitutions are alike, and so there are different forms of constitutional government according to the way in which a constitution determines the distribution of power among the offices of government. That, in turn, is determined by the purpose or ultimate objective to be served by the government being constituted. Jefferson calls attention to the relation between the form to be chosen and the purpose to be served by immediately qualifying the phrase "in such form" by the further phrase "as to them shall seem most likely to effect their safety and happiness."

"As to them shall seem most likely to effect . . ." These words, especially the words "shall seem most likely" forecast the debates that were to occur once independence had been declared, debates concerning the form of government that the people of the individual states would select; debates in the Constitutional Convention of 1787 concerning the form of government to be set up for the *United* States; debates antecedent to the ratification of the proposed constitution; debates after ratification, and continuing to the present day, about the adequacy of that constitution for the nation's appointed ends.

That so much debate should occur is foreshadowed in Jefferson's very careful diction—"as to them shall *seem* most *likely*." He is making use of the distinction, coming down from Plato, between knowledge and opinion, between judgments having certitude and commanding agreement and merely probable judgments about which men can reasonably disagree. Jefferson's second paragraph had begun with the words "We hold these truths." He did not write: "We hold the following opinions." According to Jefferson, certitude was attainable on the level of principles. The propositions about human equality, about inalienable rights, about the requirement that government must aim to secure these rights in order to be just—these propositions were for him matters of knowledge, not of opinion. About these he thought reasonable men could not reasonably disagree. From other writings of Jefferson, we know that he would have included among such propositions the assertion that to be fully just a government has to be constitutional in form and democratic in principle. But how a constitution should be drafted, how the powers of government should be organized to embody these principles and serve these purposes, such matters Jefferson readily acknowledged belonged in the realm of "likely" opinion rather than knowledge. Reasonable men, for example, have disagreed and continue to disagree about the presidential as contrasted with the parliamentary system of constitutional government. Either, it can be argued, might "effect their safety and happiness."

The revolutionary leaders were well versed in the theories about the forms of government and acquainted with the historical fate that had befallen each of the several forms. Less than a generation earlier, most of them had been fervent admirers of the British version of the ancient form known as "mixed government," or in the words of Bracton and Fortescue, a *regimen regale et politicum,* a government both royal and constitutional. However, they had more recently come, with Bolingbroke and the Radical Whigs in the mother country, to think that that form was being subverted in Britain, in consequence of which many of the arbitrary acts of which the colonists complained had been committed. In the light of such acquaintance with the past and their own recent experiences, they were not likely to consider the problem of deciding on a form of government an easy one. In both state and national constitutional conventions, there would be ample room for reasonable differences of opinion.

It has already been suggested that Jefferson did not think the right to alter or abolish an existing form of government should be exercised impetuously or arbitrarily. Its exercise would call for a judgment made after careful deliberation. The Declaration proceeds to consider the manner in which such a judgment should be reached and the kind of evidence it would require in order to be reasonable and sober, not hasty or impetuous. It cannot be properly made unless it is prudently made.

> Prudence, indeed, will dictate that governments long established should not be changed for light and transient causes; ...

For the beginning of this section of the Declaration, Jefferson chose the venerable term "prudence." From the Greeks on, the traditional account of the four cardinal virtues had included prudence, or practical wisdom, along with fortitude, temperance, and justice. Prudence and these other virtues were, of course, first thought of as elements in the moral character of the individual person. The prudent man is one who has acquired the habit, or the firm, reliable disposition, to make judgments that are practically sound or wise. Analogically, however, in the political order, prudence can be attributed to men as rulers or as ruled, and to a whole people engaged in considering a change in government.

"Will dictate . . ." Prudence not only habituates and strengthens the mind for the process of due deliberation about the means to be chosen for an end in view under the complex circumstances of a particular time and place, but also brings practical deliberation to a close with a *dictamen* to the will. One of Thomas Paine's many ringing sentences in *Common Sense* had been: "The time for debate is over."

"That governments long established . . ." The requirements of prudence might be less onerous with regard to governments of recent date and short duration. They would not call for the respect due to governments having a protracted continuity, a long tradition, and an assured stability.

"Should not be changed for light and transient causes . . ." A decision to change—to alter or abolish—a form of government would not be prudent if the grievances to be redressed or the injustice to be rectified were not grave, long-standing, and unlikely soon to

dwindle and vanish. It is only after a people has suffered a long train of abuses and failed to halt them by civil dissent or by petitions for redress of its grievances that it is entitled to resort to more drastic measures.

> ... and, accordingly, all experience hath shown, that mankind are more disposed to suffer, while evils are sufferable, than to right themselves by abolishing the forms to which they are accustomed.

The record of human experience, showing extraordinary patience under sufferable evils, tends to confirm the recommendation of prudence which urges caution in changing governments. Jefferson, himself by temperament a revolutionary in *his* sense of the term, reveals some passion about the way that the force of custom restrains people who have been wronged from "righting" themselves. Custom is conservative and imposes a laggard pace on moral and political progress.

There is textual evidence for the belief that Jefferson had, either at hand or firmly in his memory, the last chapter of John Locke's *Second Treatise of Civil Government,* entitled "Of the Dissolution of Government." On the point here being considered, Locke had written somewhat more expansively as follows:

> It will be said that the people being ignorant and always discontented, to lay the foundation of government in the unsteady opinion and uncertain humor of the people, is to expose it to certain ruin; and no government will be able long to subsist if the people may set up a new legislative whenever they take offense at the old one. To this I answer, quite the contrary. People are not so easily got out of their old forms as some are apt to suggest. They are hardly to be prevailed with to amend the acknowledged faults in the frame they have been accustomed to. And if there be any original defects, or adventitious ones introduced by time or corruption, it is not an easy thing to get them changed, even when all the world sees there is an opportunity for it. This slowness and aversion in the people to quit their old constitutions ...

Jefferson's whole sentence, beginning with "Prudence dictates," served to remind Americans, and to inform a candid world, that the American Revolution was not a wild eruptive event, inflamed by uncontrollable passions. Many historians of the American Revolution have called it "a *conservative* revolution." In spite of the apparent contradictoriness of that phrase, it does emphasize the contention that there had been patient sufferance of evils, that protracted debate and due deliberation had taken place, that right up to the end petitions had been submitted for the redress of grievances, and that the decision to act had been prudently made after the British had evidenced their intention to resort to force.

Before reaching the concrete bill of particulars—the circumstances calling for a decision to be made—Jefferson added one more complex sentence that served to complete the general philosophical argument.

> But, when a long train of abuses and usurpations, pursuing invariably the same object, evinces a design to reduce them under absolute despotism, it is their right, it is their duty, to throw off such government, and to provide new guards for their future security.

It is useful, once again, to quote from the corresponding but more ample section of Locke's chapter on the dissolution of government:

> Such revolutions happen not upon every little mismanagement in public affairs. Great mistakes in the ruling part, many wrong and inconvenient laws, and all the slips of human frailty will be born by the people without mutiny or murmur. *But if a long train of abuses, prevarications, and artifices, all tending the same way, make the design visible to the people,* and they cannot feel what they lie under, and see whither they are going, it is not to be wondered that they should then rouse themselves, and endeavor to put the rule into such hands which may secure to them the ends for which government was at first erected.

"It is their right . . ." Quite apart from the fact that Jefferson is perforce writing with much greater compression than Locke, he is more severe in his statement of the point. Where Locke states empirically that "it is not be wondered" what people will do under the circumstances both he and Jefferson are alluding to, Jefferson speaks juridically of what it is the people's *right* to do. In the preceding sentence beginning with "Prudence dictates," as well as in the present long and complex sentence, Jefferson plainly manifests his view that we must distinguish between the *possession* of a right

and the *exercise* of it. We must also distinguish between having reasons of prudence for *not* exercising a right (which we continue to possess even when we do not exercise it) and having the *duty* to exercise that right under a given set of circumstances. It is here that Jefferson proceeds to make a moral judgment not to be found in Locke.

"It is their duty . . ." Confronted with convincing evidence of a design to subject them to despotic rule, it is the *duty* of a people to exercise their right of revolution. The duty is an elementary one. Subjugation by despotism robs a people of the exercise of its right to self-rule. Submission to subjugation ends the political life of a people. A people, then, has more than a right not to be subjugated, a right to self-government. It has a self-preserving duty to fight for its political existence as a people.

"To throw off such government, and to provide new guards for their future security." Once again, as earlier, Jefferson is careful to proceed directly from reference to the act of abolishing a government to a mention of the intention to institute a new government. A revolution is a change in the form of government, not a return to the state of nature or to anarchy. Jefferson's phrasing here of the ultimate aim of the revolution—"to provide new guards for their future security"—must be read as a variant of the earlier statement of ultimate purpose. Except for stylistic reasons, he could have repeated earlier diction and said: "to institute a new government better designed to secure the rights to life, liberty, and the pursuit of happiness."

From the foregoing sequence of general propositions in political philosophy, Jefferson drew the major premise for the Declaration's basic syllogism or line of argument. It can be formulated as follows: A PEOPLE SUBJECT TO A DESIGN OF DESPOTISM HAS THE RIGHT AND THE DUTY TO THROW OFF A GOVERNMENT EVINCING SUCH A DESIGN.

The Declaration goes on:

> Such has been the patient sufferance of these colonies. . . . The history of the present King of Great Britain is a history of repeated injuries and usurpations, all having, in direct object, the establishment of an absolute tyranny over these states.

That passage, in effect, provides the minor premise in the argument, an assertion of the following statement of fact: THE AMERICAN PEOPLE HAS BEEN SUBJECT TO SUCH A DESIGN OF DESPOTISM. An interpolated passage then reads as follows:

> . . . and such is now the necessity which constrains them to alter their former systems of government.

In effect, this passage states the conclusion of the syllogism, to which the preceding line of reasoning has led: THE AMERICAN PEOPLE, THEREFORE, HAS THE RIGHT AND THE DUTY TO THROW OFF A GOVERNMENT EVINCING SUCH A DESIGN.

What remains to be offered is evidence in support of the factual minor premise, the assertion that the American people have been subject to a design of despotism. The bill of particulars indicting the King provides that evidence. The passage in which this is accomplished begins as follows:

> To prove this, let facts be submitted to a candid world: . . .

After twenty-seven specific charges, the passage ends as follows:

> A prince, whose character is thus marked by every act which may define a tyrant, is unfit to be the ruler of a free people.

The twenty-seven charges are to be taken together as evincing "a design to reduce them under absolute despotism" and as "having, in direct object, the establishing of an absolute tyranny over these states."

Jefferson does mention the "character" of the King, but that was, perhaps, something of a slip. Neither he nor any of the revolutionary leaders would, by that time, have had any interest in the inner life of George III. The focus of the indictment was on the objective record of "a long train of abuses and usurpations." It made little difference whether these had been committed by the King or committed by his Parliament and sanctioned by him. Though there were a few covert references to Parliament, the King was the sole object of the indictment because, prior to July 4, 1776, the revolutionary leaders had come to deny that the King's Parliament in England had any authority over the colonies. Each of the colonies was presumed to have its own form of parliament or general assembly, all coequal with the British Parliament under the King. Hence the present action had to be construed as one of withdrawing allegiance to the King.

The intention of the indictment, with its twenty-seven charges, must be clearly understood. Its aim is to impeach the King and, in accordance with Locke's conception of the matter, to declare him the real rebel—the usurper who has gone beyond his constitutional prerogatives and resorted to force. Since there was no competent legal tribunal before which the charges could be placed, the indictment must be what Jefferson called it—"an appeal to the tribunal of the world."

In form, the indictment is a presentation of charges that would justify impeachment. In acts committed or sanctioned by him, the King is charged with diverse, repeated, and grave violations of the British constitution and of the rights of British citizens in America. Allegiance or consent is, therefore, to be withdrawn because these violations were destructive of the ends for which allegiance or consent had been given. Juridical impeachment being impossible, the only practical alternatives were submission to despotism or a struggle for independence.

With ample time for composition, Jefferson might well have borrowed, and used in compressed phrasing, another theme from the final chapter of Locke's treatise. In that chapter, on the dissolution of government, Locke had reiterated the proposition that rulers who usurped powers not authorized by law and so have acted unconstitutionally, ruling by force rather than by law, were properly to be designated "rebels." The people who took up arms in defense of their constitutional rights and liberties were not the rebels, but rather those who had breached the civil peace and returned to the state of war. A number of passages from Locke are worth quoting because of their relevance to the "rebellion" involving George III, on the one hand, and the American colonists, on the other.

> Whenever the legislators endeavor . . . to reduce [the people] to slavery under arbitrary power, they put themselves *into a state of war* with the people, who are thereupon absolved from any further obedience, and are left to the common refuge which God hath provided for all men against force and violence.

For rebellion being an opposition, not to persons, but authority, which is founded only in the constitutions and laws of the government: those, whoever they be, who, by force, break through, and, by force, justify their violation of them, are *truly and properly rebels* . . . those who set up force again in opposition to the laws do *rebellare*—that is, bring back again the state of war, and are properly rebels.

When . . . legislators act contrary to the *end* for which they were *constituted,* those who are [thus] guilty are guilty of *rebellion.*

[Those who introduce] a power which the people hath not authorised, actually introduce *a state of war, which is that of force without authority.*

[Those who put] themselves into a state of war with those who made them the protectors and guardians of their peace . . . are properly, and with the greatest aggravation, *rebellantes,* rebels.

Whosoever uses force without right . . . puts himself into a state of war with those against whom he so uses it, and in that state all former ties are cancelled, all other rights cease, and every one has a right to defend himself, and to *resist* the aggressor.

George III had declared the colonies in a state of rebellion and had begun to wage war against them. In Locke's terms, the counter proposition provides a more accurate description of the events. By the actions listed in the Declaration's indictment, the King had put himself, as well as those in Great Britain who acquiesced in his actions, into a state of war with the American colonists. He, the King, was the rebel. He had evinced a design to subject the Americans to absolute despotism—despotism being defined in exactly the same terms Locke had employed to define a "state of war"; namely, *the use of force without authority.* The only alternatives open to the Americans were submission to despotism or what Locke calls "rightful resistance"—*resistance, not rebellion.* The King was the rebel. Successful resistance to the King's rebellious acts would, however, lead to a revolution, that is, to a change in the form of government.

The substance of the twenty-seven-point indictment has been much examined. Questions have been raised about its fairness to the King, the accuracy of several of the charges, even about the intensity of the crisp phrasing. Careful scholarship with regard to such questions will always be in order; but there can be no question that Jefferson worked with the stringency of a lawyer preparing a bill of impeachment. When all reservations are taken into account, the indictment retains its full force. Each of the charges has been acknowledged to have some basis in fact. The force of the indictment derives from the cumulative or aggregate effect of the many charges.

The testamentary value of the indictment lies in the fact that the long list of wrongs reveals a rich lode of rights. The intensity of the outrage felt on so many counts arose from a keen sensitivity to the various rights, both substantive and procedural, that secure the life of a free people. It was ironic that this sensitivity on the colonists' part owed so much to their love of the venerable traditions of the "mother country."

After a strongly worded paragraph that reviewed the ineffectual appeals made by the colonists to their "British brethren" for their support of the American cause, the Declaration goes on to state the action that now must be taken to carry out the conclusion reached in the foregoing argument.

> **We, therefore, the representatives of the united States of America . . . in the name, and by the authority of the good people of these colonies, solemnly publish and declare, that *these united colonies are, and of right ought to be, free and independent states; that they are absolved from all allegiance to the British Crown, and that all political connection between them and the state of Great Britain is, and ought to be, totally dissolved;* . . .**

The action is taken by the representatives of the *United States of America* (the first official use of this phrase), *in the name* and *by the authority of the good people of these colonies.* The italicized part of the text above was inserted by the Continental Congress, altering what Jefferson had written. It was taken from Lee's Resolution of Independence, which had been approved by Congress on July 2. Congress also inserted into Jefferson's draft the "appeal to the Supreme Judge of the world for the rectitude of our intentions," and the phrase in the last sentence—"with a firm reliance on the protection of Divine Providence."

> . . . and that, as free and independent states, they
> have full power to levy war, conclude peace, con-
> tract alliances, establish commerce, and to do all
> other acts and things which independent states may
> of right do.

Once again, the Declaration does not rest content with the act of
dissolving existing political connections. Once again, having in
mind the intent to assume an equal station among the powers of the
earth, the united states describe themselves not merely as separated
from Great Britain, but also as having the status of a free and
independent people, ready to exercise the sovereign powers possessed by their peers among the nations of the earth.

> **And, for the support of this declaration, with a firm
> reliance on the protection of Divine Providence, we
> mutually pledge to each other our lives, our for-
> tunes, and our sacred honor.**

The mutual pledge looked immediately to the ordeal of the war
for independence. Beyond that, it looked forward to what this
people might be held accountable for in human history, after their
independence had been won by military victory. Whatever constitutional difficulties were later to arise concerning the bonds of
union which united these states, it was as united that they went to
war and looked forward to a united life after the war.

Later controversies about the juridical character of "the union"
adverted to this final paragraph in the Declaration. We learn, for
example, from James Madison's reports on the Constitutional Convention, that James Wilson held the view that, during the war, the
states formed one community; that when the colonies became
independent of Great Britain, they did not thereby become independent of each other; that for him the Declaration of Independence provided the basis for the proposition that the several states
that had adopted that measure were independent in their confeder-
ated character, not as separate communities.

Reference to the Declaration was also pivotal for the impassioned argument by John Quincy Adams in 1839, in an address

delivered by him in more ominous times, celebrating the fiftieth anniversary of George Washington's inauguration. The address was entitled "The Declaration and the Constitution." It contained the following passage:

> It is not immaterial to remark that the signers of the Declaration, though qualifying themselves as the representatives of the United States of America, in general Congress assembled, yet issue the Declaration *in the name and by the authority of the good people of the colonies;* and that they declare, *not* each of separate colonies but the *united colonies,* free and independent states. The *whole people* declared the colonies *in their united condition* of right, free, and independent states.

Within a generation after that address, the idea of "union" was to become a tragic theme.

The Preamble to the Constitution of the United States

WE, THE PEOPLE OF THE UNITED STATES, in order to form a more perfect union, establish justice, insure domestic tranquility, provide for the common defense, promote the general welfare, and secure the blessings of liberty to ourselves and our posterity, do ordain and establish this Constitution for the United States of America.

The Preamble to the Constitution of the United States

> We, the people of the United States, in order to form
> a more perfect union, establish justice, insure domes-
> tic tranquility, provide for the common defense, pro-
> mote the general welfare, and secure the blessings of
> liberty to ourselves and our posterity, do ordain and
> establish this Constitution for the United States of
> America.

THIS beautifully constructed, lucid sentence poses direct questions to any commentator—questions about the nature of the action taken, its agent, its purpose, its beneficiary.

The address to such questions, however, must first take account of the fact that the sentence issued from a convention and must take account of the ideas that led to the invention of such an instrument. Gordon S. Wood, a historian, has firmly shown that "the Americas' refined conception of a constitution did not at once spring into being everywhere with Independence . . . and so, too, the instrument of the constitutional convention was only awkwardly and unevenly developed." The importance of the distinctively American practical invention of a constitutional convention is stressed by historians who are concerned with the emergence of American constitutionalism as a novel political departure.[1]

[1] See Andrew G. McLaughlin, *The Foundations of American Constitutionalism,* Chapter 4; R. R. Palmer, *The Age of the Democratic Revolution,* Chapter VIII; and Gordon S. Wood, *The Creation of the American Republic, 1776–1787,* Chapters VII and VIII.

A brief indication of their discoveries is pertinent here in order to explain the precise meaning of the phrase "We the people" (the grammatical subject of the Preamble's elegant single sentence) as well as the significance of "do ordain and establish" (the grammatical predicate describing the action taken).

> We, the people . . . do ordain and establish . . .

Even before the Declaration of Independence, revolutionary leaders in some of the colonies had spoken of the need to rethink their governments. The Declaration of Independence, insistently and with great care, spoke not just of the right to overthrow bad government, but of the people's right to "institute new government." In the late spring of 1775, Massachusetts petitioned the Continental Congress for "explicit advice respecting the taking up and exercising the powers of civil government." In his autobiography John Adams recalled his part in the response of Congress to that petition:

> We must realize the theories of the wisest writers and invite the people to erect the whole building with their own hands upon the broadest foundation. That this could be done only by conventions of the representatives chosen by the people in the several colonies, in the most exact proportions. That it was my opinion that Congress ought now to recommend to the people of every colony to call such conventions immediately and set up governments of their own, under their own authority, for the people were the source of all authority and original of all power. These were new, strange, and terrible doctrines to the greatest part of the members, but not a very small number heard them with apparent pleasure.

Later in the fall of 1775, when New Hampshire similarly petitioned the Congress, John Adams continued the argument:

> Although the opposition was still inveterate, many members of Congress began to hear me with more patience, and some began to ask civil questions: How can the people institute governments?
>
> My answer was: By conventions of representatives, freely, fairly, and proportionally chosen.
>
> When the convention has fabricated a government, or a constitution rather, how do we know the people will submit to it?
>
> If there is any doubt of that, the convention may send out their

project of a constitution to the people in their several towns, counties, or districts, and the people may make the acceptance of it their own act.

As early, then, as 1775, John Adams appeared to have a firm hold on the idea of the people as the constituent power.

However, the idea was far from clearly grasped in the colonies at large. Despite the confusions and anxieties attending the initiation of the war of independence, the colonies did proceed, in one or another way, to turn themselves into independent commonwealths or states. Eight colonies did so in 1776. Two more followed in 1777. Rhode Island and Connecticut, for reasons of no importance here, stayed with their old charters.

Massachusetts was very late. It did not give itself a new constitution until 1780. The reasons for the delay are of decisive importance in the whole story.

Andrew C. McLaughlin speaks of "the establishment of State governments" as the "dramatic and conclusive proclamation of independence." Yet he acknowledges that the method by which they were instituted, except in the case of Massachusetts, was murky to a degree. The work of instituting new governments was done by existing governments—the assemblies or provincial congresses that were *de facto* in power. Their documents came from the exercise of that *de facto* power. To be sure, they were "thought of," McLaughlin says, "as more or less coming from the people and expressing popular will." But they had not issued from a body of men expressly assigned by the people to institute new governments. In most cases, their work took effect without any sort of submission to a popular vote. And, in one way or another, the *de facto* governmental bodies stayed on as the new governments.

The establishment of new state governments in such troubled times was impressive and important. But the procedures were not sound if they are measured by "the idea of the people as the constituent power." That idea, which R. R. Palmer speaks of as "distinctively American," was a practical idea, an idea calling for a method of action. The distinctiveness lay in its institutionalizing of old doctrines—in its bringing to effective, symbolic, and historical actuality doctrines about the sovereignty of the people, about the people as the original fount of all power in governments, about authority as transmitted from the consent of the governed, about a fundamental law antecedent to government because constitutive of government, a law different in kind and in force from the statutes that would issue from the constituted government.

Palmer concedes that, though it was surely "adumbrated" in Jefferson's phrase in the Declaration about "instituting new governments," the idea "developed unclearly, gradually, and sporadically." He concedes that in none of the ten states that gave themselves new constitutions in 1776 and 1777 "did a true constituent convention meet, and, as it were, calmly and rationally devise government out of a state of nature." In those states, the procedures did not clearly distinguish existing from constituent bodies or statutory law from fundamental law, and failed for the most part to engage "the people" in the process of instituting new governments.

In Massachusetts, the story was different. It is worth a brief retelling here, if it is true that the idea of the people as a constituent power is an important part of the American Testament, and true that the idea found historical maturity in Massachusetts. Palmer tells the first part of the story:

The revolutionary leadership in Massachusetts, including both the Adamses, was quite satisfied to be rid of the British, and otherwise to keep the Bay State as it had always been. They therefore "resumed" the charter of 1691. . . . [However], demands were heard for a new constitution. It was said that the charter of 1691 was of no force, since the royal power that had issued it was no longer valid. It was said that no one could be governed without his consent, and that no living person had really consented to this charter. Some Berkshire towns even hinted that they did not belong to Massachusetts at all until they shared in constituting the new commonwealth. . . . "The law to bind all must be assented to by all," declared the farmers of Sutton.[2]

[2] Students of the Western constitutionalist tradition can construe this proposition from the farmers of Sutton, as almost a translation of a maxim of medieval constitutionalism. In his *Lectures on Law,* delivered at the College of Philadelphia in 1790–1791, James Wilson, America's leading jurist, adverted to this medieval maxim: "Let us next pay the respect, which is due to the celebrated sentiment of the English Justinian, Edward the First. Lex justissima, ut quod omnes tangit, ab omnibus approbetur. *It is a most just law, that what affects all should be approved by all.* This golden rule is, with great propriety, inserted in his summons to his parliament." The farmers of Sutton urged an application of this maxim in a context where the people, rather than a King, was sovereign.

. . . It began to seem that a constitution was necessary not only to secure liberty but to establish authority, not only to protect the individual but to found the state.

In the fall of 1776, the Massachusetts provincial congress resolved to consider making a new constitution. It issued an appeal to the towns for a grant of authority to the General Court for that work. In a town hall meeting, the people of Concord responded as follows:

A meeting of the inhabitants (free men and twenty-one years of age and older) of the town of Concord met by adjournment on October 21, 1776, to take into consideration a resolve of the honorable House of Representatives of this state made on September 17. The town resolved as follows:

Resolve 1. This state being presently destitute of a *properly established* form of government, it is absolutely necessary that a government should be immediately formed and established.

Resolve 2. The supreme legislature, either in its proper capacity or in a joint committee, is by no means a body proper to form and establish a constitution or form a government, for the following reasons:

First, because we conceive that a constitution in its proper idea intends a system of principles established to secure the subject in the possession and enjoyment of their rights and privileges against any encroachments of the governing part.

Second, because the same body that forms a constitution has a power to alter it.

Third, because a constitution alterable by the supreme legislature is no security at all to the subject against any encroachment of the governing part on any or on all of their rights and privileges.

Resolve 3. It appears highly necessary and expedient to this town that a convention or congress be immediately chosen to form and establish a constitution by the inhabitants of the respective towns in this state. . . .

Resolve 4. When the convention or congress has formed a constitution, they are to adjourn for a short time and publish their proposed constitution for the inspection of the inhabitants of this state.

Resolve 5. The honorable House of Assembly of this state desires to recommend to the inhabitants of the state to proceed to choose a convention or congress for the purpose abovesaid as soon as possible.

This remarkable set of Concord "resolves" firmly and maturely holds the idea of the people as constituent power. However, the suggestions of the Concord meeting did not at first prevail. The House, through the General Court, enacted a constitution in 1778. It was rejected by a five-to-one majority of the towns—for various reasons, including its lack of a bill of rights; its failure to eliminate slavery; its attaching a property qualification to the voting right; *and also* because it had not been drafted by a body separate from the government.

By June of 1779, however, Concord did prevail. The General Court issued an order for a special election in which all towns were to choose delegates to a state convention, having as "its sole purpose the forming of a new constitution." John Adams, who had been the counselor to the whole nation on the instituting of new state governments, was at the Massachusetts state convention. However, this time he sat, not as a major leader in the *de facto* government of the provincial congress, but as a delegate sent to the special state constitutional convention by the electorate of Braintree, Massachusetts.

Needless to say, Adams was a member of the drafting committee. His draft met with only one important emendation in the convention. The constitution that came from the convention was ratified by the towns, and it became the Constitution of the Commonwealth of Massachusetts in 1780. Its shape and several provisions were of major importance to the deliberations of the 1787 convention in Philadelphia.

The importance of the emendation that the convention made in Adams's draft is stressed by Palmer:

In the enacting clause [of his draft] of the preamble, Adams wrote: "We, therefore, the delegates of the people of Massachusetts . . . agree upon the following . . . Constitution of the Commonwealth of Massachusetts." The convention made a significant emendation: "*We,* therefore, *the people* of Massachusetts . . . agree upon, ordain and establish . . ." The formula, *We the people ordain and establish,* expressing the developed theory of the people as constituent power, was used for the first time in the Massachusetts constitution of 1780, whence it passed into the preamble of the United States constitution of 1787 and the new Pennsylvania constitution of 1790, after which it became common in the constitutions of the *new* states, and in new constitutions of the old states. Adams did not invent the formula. He was content with the matter-of-fact or purely empirical statement that the "delegates" had "agreed." It was the popularly elected convention that rose to more abstract heights. Providing in advance for popular ratification, it imputed the creation of government to the people.

The emendation, so construed, supports the contention of Andrew C. McLaughlin that "by their words and acts the constitution-makers of Massachusetts *made actual* the theory of the origin of government in the will of the people."

During the period when the Articles of Confederation were in force, clarity about the people's constituent power became more widespread. In South Carolina, there was increasing dissatisfaction with the "new constitution" that had been adopted in 1778 by the sitting Revolutionary Congress, even without a new election. In the South Carolina discussion, there appeared in 1784 a pamphlet, *Conciliatory Hints,* written by Thomas Tudor Tucker. Gordon S. Wood calls Tucker's pamphlet "one of the most prescient and remarkable pamphlets written in the Confederation period." Wood presents the pertinent passages:

"All authority [Tucker writes] is derived from the people at large, held only during their pleasure, and exercised only for their benefit. . . . No man has any privilege above his fellow-citizens, except whilst in office, and even then, none but what they have thought proper to vest in him, solely for the purpose of supporting him in the effectual performance of his duty to the public." Therefore, "the privileges of the legislative branches ought to be defined by the constitution and should be fixed as low as is consistent with the public welfare." South Carolina needed a new Constitution. The old one "(if such it may be called)" should be amended by convening the people in accord with "the true principles of equal freedom" that were being accepted by almost all Americans in the 1780's, thereby fixing the Constitution "on the firm and proper foundation of the express consent of the people, unalterable by the legislature, or any other authority but that by which it is to be framed." Only such a constitution based on this "undeniable authority" of the collective people would be something "more than the will of the legislature" and therefore "would have the most promising chance of stability." Then, in a brilliant passage, Tucker summed up what Americans had done in two decades to the conception of a constitution: "The constitution should be the avowed act of the people at large. It should be the first and fundamental law of the State, and should prescribe the limits of all delegated power. It should be declared to be paramount to all acts of the Legislature, and irrepealable and unalterable by any authority but the express consent of a majority of the citizens collected by such regular mode as may be therein provided."

Such things as the Concord Resolutions, the Massachusetts constituent procedures of 1779–80, and Tucker's powerful pamphlet prepared the way for the use, in the Preamble to the Constitution of the United States, of the phrase "We, the people of the United States" to designate the enacting agent of the constitutive act.

Two major actions taken in the Philadelphia Convention, both of them in a way "illegal," all but necessitated that way of designating the source of the enactment.

The Resolution of Congress that called the Philadelphia Convention into existence spoke of "the revision of the Articles of Confederation" as the Convention's "sole and express purpose." Early in the Convention, the members, relying on the fact that the stated object of that revision was "to form a more perfect union," in effect scrapped the Articles of Confederation and proceeded toward the framing of a radically different kind of constitution. In *Federalist #15,* Hamilton called attention to the pivot of this radical change:

> The great and radical vice in the construction of the existing Confederation is in the principle of legislation for states or governments, in their corporate or collective capacities, and as contradistinguished from the individuals of which they consist. . . . [But] if we still will adhere to the design of a national government . . . we must resolve to incorporate into our plan those ingredients which may be considered as forming the characteristic difference between a *league* and a *government;* we must extend the authority of the Union to the persons of the citizens—the only proper objects of government.

The actions of the new national government were to exert their effect directly on the individual citizens. The words of the Sutton farmers became pertinent: "The law to bind all must be assented to by all." *A fortiori,* the fundamental law—instituting government, with assigned powers and purposes—should be assented to by all. The Convention did not fail to follow through on the logic of popular sovereignty. It called for special ratifying conventions, thus bypassing the state legislatures. In *Federalist #40*, Madison flatly conceded the "illegality" of this action:

> In one particular it is admitted that the convention . . . departed from the tenor of their commission. Instead of reporting a plan requiring confirmation of the legislatures of all the States, they have reported a plan which is to be confirmed by the people, and may be carried into effect by nine States only.

In *Federalist #22*, Hamilton directly defended the change in the mode of ratification:

> It has not a little contributed to the infirmities of the existing federal system [i.e., under the Articles of Confederation], that it never had a ratification by the people. Resting on no better foundation than the consent of the several legislatures, it has been exposed to frequent and intricate questions concerning the validity of its powers, and has, in some instances, given birth to the enormous doctrine of a right to legislative repeal. Owing its ratification to the law of a State, it has been contended that the same authority might repeal the law by which it was ratified. However gross a heresy it may be to maintain that a party to a compact has the right to revoke that compact, the doctrine itself has had respectable advocates. The possibility of a question of this nature proves the necessity of laying the foundations of our national government deeper than in the mere sanction of delegated authority. The fabric of American empire ought to rest on the solid basis of the consent of the people. The streams of national power ought to flow immediately from that pure, original fountain of all legitimate authority.

In effect, the Grand Convention pressed for constitutive procedures, like those used in Massachusetts in 1780, that would conform to and confirm the doctrines about the people as the source of authority in government. If the new national government was "to carry its agency to the person of the citizens," then its legitimation would have to come from the persons whom that government was to touch.

The decision that ratification had to come from people's conventions, assembled for that special purpose, subjected the constitution that issued from Philadelphia to general, widespread argument. Patrick Henry, speaking in the Virginia ratifying convention against ratification, said: "What right had they to say, 'We, the people'?

My political curiosity, exclusive of my anxious solicitude for the public welfare, leads me to ask—Who authorized them to speak the language of 'We, the people,' instead of, 'We, the states'? States are the characteristics and the soul of a confederation. If the states be not *the agents of this compact,* it must be one great, consolidated, national government of the people of all the states."

Edmund Pendleton, for ratification, answered him: "But an objection is made to the form: the expression 'We, the people' is thought improper. Permit me to ask the gentleman who made this objection, who but the people can delegate powers? Who but the people have a right to form government? The expression is a common one, and a favorite one with me. . . . If the objection be that the Union ought to be not of the people but of the state governments, then I think the choice of the former very happy and proper. What have the state governments to do with it? Were they to determine, the people would not, in that case, be the judges upon what terms it was adopted."

The Declaration of Independence had been issued by the *United* States after an argument of the people as a whole with Great Britain, as well as an argument among the peoples of the several States. The struggle for ratification was also to be an argument. When both arguments were concluded, the Revolution was consummated. The nation was independent *and* it had instituted a new government.

James Madison, "the father of the Constitution," epitomized the event in almost emblematic style: "In Europe, charters of liberty have been granted by power. America has set the example of charters of power granted by liberty."

The American people, it has become commonplace to say, venerate their Constitution. More worthy of veneration, perhaps, than its actual provisions is the manner of its making.

What has been said in these few pages about "We, the people of the United States," about the people's constituent power, and about appropriate procedures for its exercise, is masterfully summarized in the prelude to John Marshall's opinion for the Court in the 1819 *M'Culloch* v. *Maryland* case—an opinion of decisive importance for the scope of federal power and for the future life of the nation.

Maryland, along with several state legislatures, laid taxes on the Second Bank of the United States. The Baltimore branch of the

United States Bank determined to ignore the state law, whereupon Maryland brought suit against its cashier, James M'Culloch. He appealed the Maryland court's decision, which had upheld the state law, to the Supreme Court. John Marshall's opinion, for the Court, reversed and found the state tax on the national bank unconstitutional.

The whole of Marshall's massive argument is not pertinent here. What is pertinent to the points that have been urged in the preceding pages is Marshall's "prelude":

In discussing this question, the counsel for the State of Maryland have deemed it of some importance, in the construction of the Constitution, to consider that instrument not as emanating from the people but as the act of sovereign and independent states. The powers of the general government, it has been said, are delegated by the states, who alone are truly sovereign; and must be exercised in subordination to the states, who alone possess supreme dominion.

It would be difficult to sustain this proposition. The Convention which framed the Constitution was indeed elected by the state legislatures. But the instrument, when it came from their hands, was a mere proposal, without obligation or pretensions to it. It was reported to the then existing Congress of the United States with a request that it might "be submitted to a Convention of Delegates, chosen in each state by the people thereof, under the recommendation of its legislature, for their assent and ratification." This mode of proceeding was adopted; and by the Convention, by Congress, and by the state legislatures the instrument was submitted to the people. They acted upon it in the only manner in which they can act safely, effectively, and wisely, on such a subject—by assembling in convention.

It is true, they assembled in their several states; and where else should they have assembled? No political dreamer was ever wild enough to think of breaking down the lines which separate the states, and of compounding the American people into one common mass. Of consequence, when they act, they act in their states. But the measures they adopt do not, on that account, cease to be the measures of the people themselves, or become the measures of the state governments.

From these conventions the Constitution derives its whole authority. The government proceeds directly from the people; is "ordained and established" in the name of the people; and is declared to be ordained "in order to form a more perfect union,

establish justice, ensure domestic tranquility, and secure the blessings of liberty" to themselves and to their posterity. The assent of
the states, in their sovereign capacity, is implied in calling a convention, and thus submitting that instrument to the people. But
the people were at perfect liberty to accept or reject it; and their
act was final. It required not the affirmance, and could not be
negatived, by the state governments. The Constitution, when thus
adopted, was of complete obligation, and bound the state sovereignties.

It has been said that the people had already surrendered all their
powers to the state sovereignties, and had nothing more to give.
But, surely, the question whether they may resume and modify
the powers granted to government does not remain to be settled
in this country. Much more might the legitimacy of the general
government be doubted had it been created by the states. The
powers delegated to the state sovereignties were to be exercised
by themselves, not by a distinct and independent sovereignty
created by themselves. To the formation of a league, such as was
the Confederation, the state sovereignties were certainly competent. But when, "in order to form a more perfect union," it was
deemed necessary to change this alliance into an effective government, possessing great and sovereign powers, and acting directly
on the people, the necessity of referring it to the people, and of
deriving its powers directly from them, was felt and acknowledged
by all.

The government of the Union, then (whatever may be the influence of this fact on the case), is emphatically and truly, a
government of the people. In form and in substance it emanates
from them. Its powers are granted by them and are to be exercised
directly on them and for their benefit.

The fortunes of history gave the American people an unprecedented opportunity to preside over its own political birth. Its birth
gave historical reality to doctrines about the sovereignty of the
people and the consent of the governed, which had hitherto lived
only in the order of reason. Those true doctrines came to be so
firmly held that there developed a determination to find exemplary
procedures whereby the import of those truths could be enacted,
acted out, historically staged. By their invention of clear and symbolic procedures, by their insistence on the proper mode of enactment, the Americans distinguished themselves. No nation had ever
so brilliantly presided over the consummation of its political birth.

A written constitution was that consummation. A constitution as law is radically different from the laws made by a legislature that the constitution sets up and to which it gives the authority to legislate. Nevertheless, it falls under the generic conception of law. A medieval statement of that conception defined law as an ordination of reason for the common good instituted by whosoever has the authority and duty to care for the community, and publicly promulgated. The lawmaker or legislator must have authority; otherwise, his edicts or prescriptions would be mere dictates of force. In the enactment of the fundamental law which is a constitution, that authority must rest with the people as a whole, for until the constitution has been enacted legislative authority cannot be legally conferred upon any person or assembly of persons. From their inherent right to self-rule, the people themselves have the authority and duty to act for the care of the community.

The lawmaker, whether the people as a whole or its authorized representatives, exercises both reason and will in the formation and enactment of a law. In the case of the fundamental law which is a constitution, the lawmaker, in formulating the provisions of the constitution, sets forth a reasoned ordination of the offices and powers required for the administration of government. Having thus *ordained* the form which the government is to take, the lawmaker, by an act of will, *establishes* its existence.

Being thus rationally formulated and voluntarily instituted or established, laws are made to serve a purpose, which is sometimes explicitly stated, sometimes not. At the end of Book IV of *The Laws,* Plato urged that every law should have a preamble stating its purpose. The medieval definition of law stated the generic purpose of any and every just law—"to serve the common good." The Preamble to the law that is the Constitution of the United States names six specific objectives which together constitute the common good that is to be served.

> . . . in order to form a more perfect union, establish justice, insure domestic tranquility, provide for the common defense, promote the general welfare, and secure the blessings of liberty to ourselves and our posterity, . . .

Before turning to those six objectives to ask questions about them, first taking them all together and then taking each of them separately, it is pertinent to ask whose objectives they are.

After the proposed constitution has been adopted and is in force as the fundamental law of the land, the objectives specified in the Preamble are ends to be served by the constituted government. The ultimate justification of any act of government, whether legislative, judicial, or executive, should in principle at least reside in the possibility of showing that it serves one or more of these objectives. However, the objectives stated in the Preamble are objectives that have been assigned to the government being created by the constitution. At the constituting moment—the point at which the constitution itself is being ordained and established by the people—the Preamble states purposes that the people themselves have for constituting a government, and a particular form of government. They do not cease to be the people's purposes when, subsequently, they become the assigned objectives of the government that the people have established.

The authority and power conferred upon the officers of government, to enable them to serve these purposes, is henceforth and always held by them as instruments or vicegerents of the people. The constitutive action by the people is not an act of abdication. The people does not "confer all its authority and power" finally and irrevocably upon the officers of government, as Justinian would have it when he formulated the juridical fiction about the transmission of power and authority from the people of Rome to the Emperor.

This is to be "a political experiment," James Madison wrote in *Federalist* #39, resting "on the capacity of mankind for self-government." It is "an experiment," Thomas Jefferson said, "to show whether man can be trusted with self-government." The people who have established a government for themselves are to remain, after that government has been established, the permanent, principal rulers; the officers of the established government function only as the transient, instrumental rulers, responsible (in the words of Lincoln) to "their masters." The people as principal rulers must continually measure the performance of their appointed representatives—their instruments of government, now in office, now out—by reference to the purposes or objectives that it had in mind when it devised this framework of government, under which they hold office for a time.

There are two other ways of making what is substantially the same point about the implications of the people's constituent act.

C. H. McIlwain, an authority on the Western constitutional tradition, emphasizes that the very idea of constitutionalism always meant *limited* government. A constitution is a fundamental law placing legal limits on the power of government. When the constitution is a written one issuing from a single constituent act, the point is fully manifest. If the transmission of authority and power was to be total and final, as in the Roman juridical fiction about the Emperor, there would be no point to a constitution. A totalitarian government has no limits; whatever pleases it has the force of law. The statement of limits in the Preamble is in terms of broad, general purposes. But their very statement as the People's purposes serves notice that this is to be limited government. The limits will be given a more determinate statement in the provisions of the Constitution, which grants and withholds certain powers.

Again, the very idea of a constitution, issuing from a people and limiting government by the very act of setting forth its organization, implies the distinction between society and the state. (The terms "the people" and "society" designate the same entity. The first term, "the people," emphasizes that a society is a whole composed of human persons who are themselves natural wholes. The second term, "society," emphasizes that the entity referred to does not have the kind of unity that a natural organism possesses; it has only a unity of order—a unity that stems from the fact that the persons who comprise the society continue to associate for a common purpose, their common good.) The distinction between society and the state is effectively destroyed by any sort of totalitarianism, in which the state, in its omnipotence and omnicompetence, uses "the people" as passive material to be molded or shaped by the state, exercising unlimited powers.

Constitutionalism maintains the distinction between society and the state. Society is an association of associations, including the family, religious associations, economic corporations, intellectual, artistic, and professional associations of many kinds, as well as the political association that is called the body politic or the state. Effective powers may be conferred upon the officers of government to achieve the objectives of the political association into which the people have entered. But the people who are members of that association are also members of other associations that have other unifying purposes, to serve which they must retain a limited autonomy in the discharge of their functions. That autonomy is

preserved only so long as the government of the political community does not intrude or encroach upon the operation of these nonpolitical associations. Government should do for the people, Lincoln
was to say later, only what the people cannot do for themselves,
either as individuals or through the various associations that they
form to serve one or another nonpolitical purpose.

The points made—about the objectives of government as the
purposes of the people who have established the government, about
the limited and instrumental character of the government thus
established, about the distinction between society and the state, and
about the relation of the political community to other forms of
human association within the society as a whole—are confirmed by
the very diction of the Preamble. The Preamble does not say, for
example, that government is being instituted for the purpose of
unifying the people of the several states, but rather for the purpose
of making such unity as already existed *more perfect.* If the people
did not antecedently possess some unity, they could not have acted
as *a* people. Similarly, if they did not antecedently have liberty, they
could not have performed the free political act of constituting a
government to serve the purpose of *securing* the blessings of liberty
to themselves and their posterity. Each such phrase—to make more
perfect, to establish, to insure, to provide for, to promote, to secure
—bears witness to the instrumental fashion of government in serving the objectives assigned.

The six objectives stated in the Preamble should first be considered in their relation to one another as elements of the common
good.

> . . . in order to form a more perfect union, establish
> justice, insure domestic tranquility, provide for the
> common defense, promote the general welfare, and
> secure the blessings of liberty to ourselves and our
> posterity, . . .

In the second paragraph of the Preamble to the Massachusetts
Constitution of 1780, John Adams wrote:

> The body politic is formed by a voluntary association of indivi
> duals; it is a social compact by which the whole people covenants
> with each citizen and each citizen with the whole people that all
> shall be governed by certain laws *for the common good.*

The word "common" in the phrase "common good," can be understood in two ways: on the one hand, as signifying goods that are common to all because they are the same for all; on the other hand, as signifying goods that are common to all because they are shared or participated in by all. The happiness which all human beings have an inalienable right to seek for themselves as individual persons is not an individual but a common good, in the sense that the elements of a good human life are the same for all, even though each individual seeks in his own way to make a good human life for himself. The domestic tranquility of a society, its unity, the justice of its laws, its self-defense or security, the general welfare, and the blessings of liberty—these, too, are not individual but common goods, in the sense that they are goods shared by or participated in by all members of the political community.

A good government is one that serves the common good in both senses of the term: in the first sense when it aims to secure for each member of the community his inalienable human rights, among which the right to seek personal happiness is principal and ultimate; in the second sense when it aims to achieve the objectives stated in the Preamble, for each of these is a good in which all members of the community can and should participate or share.

The Declaration of Independence states the ultimate objective to be achieved by a just government. The Preamble states objectives that serve as means to that ultimate objective; for without the elements of the shared common good specified in the Preamble, the individual persons who compose the political community cannot effectively engage in the pursuit of happiness. Just as they must have their lives and liberties protected as conditions indispensable for living well, so they must enjoy the unity, and peace or tranquility of civil society, a civil society in which justice is done, in which political liberty prevails, and in which the general welfare is promoted—for without these things, they will be impeded or frustrated in their efforts to live well. The reason for their association in a political community is to secure for themselves these common goods so indispensable to their pursuit of happiness.

When the phrase "common good" is used in the singular, it embraces, as elements of itself, the plural common goods specified in the Preamble. The six objectives assigned to government by the Preamble provide us with an articulation of the all-embracing and complex common good. The six purposes, though clearly distinct, must be related to one another; they are like parts of an organic whole, not discrete items in a mere aggregation or collection.

The assertion that no society worth living in can exist without unity, justice, peace, self-defense, welfare, and liberty does not preclude what might well be an extended set of problematic interrelations—no unity without justice; no domestic tranquility without justice; no welfare without justice; no liberty without justice; or no justice without unity, order, and peace; or no justice without liberty; or no domestic tranquility without justice; and so on. Given that kind of tension in the interrelations of the six, grave errors of emphasis are certainly conceivable and even likely to occur. For example, an inordinate devotion to public tranquility (lately called "law and order") might become a threat to justice; an inordinate desire to have the general welfare promoted might threaten liberties; an inordinate devotion to liberties might hamper doing justice; an inordinate concern for the common defense (lately called "national security") might subvert the concern for justice and for liberty.

The suggestion is not only that the political life of the nation should be assessed by reference to the way in which we have implemented the six purposes stated in the Preamble, but also that the constitutional history of the nation should be examined for mistakes of policy in trying to achieve one or another of these objectives at the expense of others.

We turn now to each of the six objectives considered by itself.

. . . in order to form a more perfect union, . . .

In the context of the Convention of 1787, there is no question about what this clause meant historically, and no question as to why it had to come first. The Convention was called because of the pervasive judgment that the Articles of Confederation had failed to bring sufficient unity to the United States, had indeed brought impotence and confusion at home, and dishonor and distrust abroad. Hence the primary motive for the calling of the convention lay in the hope that means could be found to bring about a more perfect union than the Articles had achieved.

The debates, in the public forum and in the ratifying conventions, centered upon the style and vigor of the union that would be served by the new Constitution. The design of a federal republic was itself a novelty. The intent—to have "an indissoluble union of indestructible, hitherto 'sovereign' states"—outran all political experience.

In the years ahead, the evocation of "the Union" was to become a kind of talisman. The major theme of Washington's noble Farewell Address was "the Union." He spoke of it reverently, but with grave apprehensions about its present state and its future. He spoke of it not just in juridical terms, but as something delicately affected —helped or harmed—by actions in every dimension of the effort at a truly national life.

The campaign leading to the election of the third President of the United States was marked by virulent hostility between the "parties" of Hamilton and Jefferson. Jefferson's First Inaugural was tense with his hope and his effort to initiate a reconciliation—to move toward the concord so necessary and so desirable. Only a few decades later, the controversy about nullification occurred. By the time of Lincoln's First Inaugural it was possible—and necessary— to assert that "a disruption of the federal Union, heretofore only menaced, is now formidably attempted."

Before leaving these brief intimations about the theme of "the Union" in our national history, some words from Lincoln's First Inaugural Address, in that ominous context, should be set down:

> I hold that, in contemplation of universal law and of the Constitution, the Union of these states is perpetual. . . . The Union is much older than the Constitution. It was formed, in fact, by the Articles of Association in 1774. It was matured and continued by the Declaration of Independence in 1776. It was further matured, and the faith of all the then thirteen states expressly plighted and engaged, that it should be perpetual by the Articles of Confederation of 1778. And finally, in 1787, one of the declared objects for ordaining and establishing the Constitution, was "to form a more perfect Union."
>
> But if destruction of the Union by one or by a part only of the states be lawfully possible, the Union is *less* perfect than before the Constitution, having lost the vital element of perpetuity.
>
> It follows from these views that no state, upon its own mere motion, can lawfully get out of the Union—that resolves and ordinances to that effect are legally void; and that acts of violence within any state or states against the authority of the United States are insurrectionary or revolutionary, according to circumstances.

I therefore consider that, in view of the Constitution and the laws, the Union is unbroken; and to the extent of my ability, I shall take care, as the Constitution itself expressly enjoins upon me, that the laws of the Union be faithfully executed in all the states. Doing this I deem to be only a simple duty on my part; and I shall perform it, so far as practicable, *unless my rightful masters, the American people,* shall withhold the requisite means or in some authoritative manner direct the contrary.

The continual, heightened concern about "the Union" in our life as a nation derives from the fact that as a matter of historical development the union originally conceived as of the States has become, and has come to be regarded as, a union also of the people. However, there are good philosophical reasons why "to form a more perfect union" should be the first item in an articulation of the common good and of the purposes of government—the first item in the preamble to *any* constitution, not just ours.

A society—a multitude of human beings associated for a common purpose and a common life—does not exist in nature as biological organisms do. It comes into existence by the voluntary actions of the human beings who decide to associate. Precisely because it originates in this way, it is said to be conventional (a thing of voluntary institution), not natural (a product of nature). But it is not purely and simply conventional.

The reason why human beings form societies (doing voluntarily what other gregarious animals do instinctively) is that men are social by nature; that is, they need to associate with their fellow men in communities in order to lead characteristically human lives. Their common purpose is the cooperative pursuit of happiness, or the mutual supplementation of their several capacities for pursuing it. Human societies, especially the family and the state or political community, are thus both natural and conventional, natural in the sense that they arise in response to a natural need, and conventional in the sense that the way in which they do arise is by rational and voluntary action rather than through the blind impulse of instinct.

In any society, especially in that most complex of all societies which is the state, government is necessary to effectuate the union of wills that brought the society into being in the first place. A government is well designed and good in performance if the way in which it directs and coordinates the life of the society instructs the associated human beings in the implications of the social ties which bind them together as one people. It should also confirm and strengthen their dedication to the objectives which they sought to achieve by willing to associate.

To whatever extent, then, the activities of an instituted government enlighten and strengthen the basic unity that gives a people its historical existence, to that extent the government is good. On the other hand, a government could have the opposite effect if, in the name of forming a more perfect union, it were to impose a rigidly uniform test of loyalty; or if, panicking about the security of the union, it were to violate liberties that were intended to be immunities from government.

. . . in order to . . . establish justice . . .

As there was a pressing need for a more perfect union, so there was an equally pressing need for the administration of justice. The authors of the *Federalist Papers,* after dealing with the question of union and with the incompetence of the Articles of Confederation in that respect, turned next to the inadequacy of the Confederation in the sphere of justice.

Alexander Hamilton, in *Federalist* #22, wrote: "A circumstance which crowns the defects of the Confederation remains yet to be mentioned—the want of a judiciary power." The Articles of Confederation contained no provisions for national courts. In Hamilton's view, the consequent domestic conflicts, confusions, and lack of uniformity in the administration of justice were intolerable. "Is it possible," he asked, "that foreign nations can either respect or confide in such a government?" The second clause in the Preamble was obviously in response to a defect in the existing state of affairs that must have been widely felt.

On the plane of more general and philosophical considerations, the second clause can be seen as following hard upon the first. Almost as important as concern for the precarious kind of unity that gives a society its very *being* is concern for the quality of the interactions among persons that give a society its *life.* It is for this reason that a constitutional government should aim at establishing justice.

Starting with Plato's *Republic* and Aristotle's *Ethics* (Book V), the consideration of the idea of justice runs through the whole tradition of Western political thought. At certain moments in that

tradition, justice is broadly conceived as encompassing three different sets of relationships: the duties or obligations that the individual
has with respect to society itself; the rights and duties that individuals have in relation to one another; and the obligations that
organized society has with respect to the rights possessed by the
human beings who are its members. These three sets of relationships, or dimensions of justice, can be denominated *contributive*
justice, *commutative* justice, and *distributive* justice.

When it is thus broadly conceived, justice can be viewed as the
overriding objective of government, one that subsumes, if it does
not include, the other objectives mentioned in the Preamble. In
Federalist #51, Madison, for example, said: "Justice is the end of
government. It is the end of civil society. It ever has been and ever
will be pursued until it be obtained, or until liberty be lost in the
pursuit."

The Declaration of Independence had spoken of a just government as one that secures to each man his inalienable rights. When
organized society, through the laws and actions of its government,
renders to its members what is rightly due them, distributive justice
is being done. Questions of justice raised about the fundamental
law of the land—the Constitution—are questions of distributive
justice. But when, in the framing of the constitution itself, the
Preamble calls for the establishment of justice, the framers have in
mind how the government being instituted must be set up to ensure
that commutative justice is done—justice in the transactions between one member of society and another. It is in this narrower
conception of justice that the establishment of justice appears to be
coordinate with the other five objectives of government stated in
the Preamble.

Commutative justice involves correlative rights and duties—
rights that one individual claims for himself and demands that
others respect, and duties on the part of others to respect those
rights—for example, an individual's right to security of life and
limb; his right against the invasion of his privacy or arbitrary
intrusion in his home; his right against defamation of character; his
rights with regard to the acquirement, accumulation, exchange, and
conveyance of property. When such rights are legally acknowledged, the laws impose upon all the obligation to respect them.
Whereas distributive justice consists in those measures by which the
state or organized society renders to each person what is rightfully

due him, commutative justice consists in one individual's rendering to another what is due him or is his by right.

In order for men to live peaceably together in society and have peaceful commerce or dealings with one another, the rights and duties which are involved in commutative justice have to be given authoritative and definitive recognition, either in immemorial customs that have the force of law or by the enactment of positive laws which prescribe or prohibit certain acts on the part of one individual in relation to another. In addition, a system of courts has to be set up to render judgments in particular cases that fall under these laws; and sanctions have to be applied for the enforcement of the decisions rendered by the courts in the resolution of litigations. To establish justice, then, a constitution must provide for legislative and judicial bodies and for agencies able to enforce the laws and the decisions of the courts.

When we turn from commutative to contributive justice, we turn from the field of private to the field of public law. Contributive justice involves other rights and wrongs than those covered by the laws of property, contract, torts; it also covers more than the wrongs prohibited by the criminal law. On the positive side, it requires that a man, in his relation to all others with whom he is associated in organized society, should render to them what he owes them in virtue of their common social nature and purpose. He owes them the contribution he can make toward the common good—toward their cooperative realization of a good human life for all. The conscientious direction of his talents to the service of society is an obligation that the virtuous man discharges. It is in this sense that Aristotle spoke of the man whose moral virtue directed him to serve the common good as exhibiting "general justice," reserving the term "special justice" to cover commutative and distributive justice.

In the period of this nation's formation, Americans had other words in their lexicon for contributive justice. "The word republic, res publica," Thomas Paine said, "means the public good, or the good of the whole." From his very rich knowledge of the literature of this period, Gordon S. Wood tells us that "no phrase except 'liberty' was invoked more often by the revolutionaries than 'the public good.'" The men of that time had learned from Montesquieu how the principle of republican government differs from that of a monarchical or despotic regime. "There is no great share of probity necessary to support a monarchical or despotic government," Montesquieu had written. "The force of laws in one, and the prince's arm in the other, are sufficient to direct and maintain the whole. But in a popular state, one spring more is necessary, namely, *virtue*" —the virtue of men as citizens, public virtue.

The men of the revolutionary-constitutional period understood that their experiment in self-government depended for its success on the people's capacity for public virtue. The concept of public virtue is identical with Aristotle's concept of contributive justice. We would today call it "public-spiritedness," and we would find it manifest in voluntary action for the common good on the part of individuals in dealing with such things as an energy shortage or widespread pollution. Our ancestors would have recognized that the task of establishing justice did not extend to this dimension of justice. They would have realized that contributive justice in the conduct of citizens must be largely left to the promptings of moral virtue on their part—largely, but not entirely, for the law does prescribe some actions for the common good, and prohibits some that are injurious to it.

The thrust of distributive justice is in the opposite direction to that of contributive justice. Contributive justice concerns the obligation of the individual to act for the good of society as a whole, an obligation that the individual is sometimes legally required to discharge, but more often discharges from moral conscience in the absence of any specific legal requirement. Distributive justice concerns what is due the individual from organized society as a whole. It aims to see that each individual shall have his fair share of the goods that only organized society can make available to all. With regard to such goods in which the members of society can share, distributive justice is done when the distribution of these goods is fairly apportioned. The doing of distributive justice is mainly covered in the Preamble under a later clause—the one that calls for the promotion of the general welfare.

. . . in order to . . . insure domestic tranquility . . .

Widely read in Western history, particularly the history of the Greek city-states and of the Roman Republic, the writers of the Preamble were thoroughly aware of the distresses to which the body politic is prone—crime and civil turmoil. They were equally cognizant of the traditional affirmation of peace—civil peace—as a component of the common good and as one of the advantages that men seek to derive from living in civil society. Their phrasing of this third objective of government echoed the language of Augustine, who had defined peace as "the tranquility of order." They probably also knew that civil peace had been spoken of as "the work of justice," at least to the extent that justice removes the obstacles to peace by removing incentives to crime and to violence in the effort to remedy grievances.

Although they are closely related, peace and justice are nevertheless distinguishable aspects of the common good. The undertaking to establish justice presumes the prevalence in the people of the personal virtue of justice, for which it seeks to provide stable arrangements through which virtuous inclinations can find orderly and effective realization. The undertaking to insure domestic tranquility attempts to ward off the prevalence of acts springing from the vice of injustice. Helping prevalent justice to find steady realization and preventing vice from becoming prevalent are, clearly enough, distinguishable even as, in public medicine, measures that promote health are distinguishable from measures to prevent disease.

Civil peace is also closely related to social union. Without the bonds of union and the tranquility of orderly life, a society would hardly exist as such and would be unable to pursue any purpose in a sustained fashion. The maintenance of peace, like the strengthening of union, is therefore to be regarded as having a certain priority to the establishment of justice, even though it is also true that the establishment of justice contributes to the maintenance of civil peace and social unity.

The leaders and people of the revolutionary generation were not so enamored of peace that they would be willing to acquiesce in any measures that might be proposed for maintaining it. They had not been willing to forgo, for the sake of peace, their rights to take whatever steps they thought necessary to redress their grievances, even steps that involved violent disturbances of the peace. In resisting British edicts and protesting against encroachments, they had often deliberately fomented domestic turbulence when their petitions for the redress of grievances went unheeded. Hence, in instituting a new government, they would perforce be sensitive to the possibility that certain measures directed to ensure domestic tranquility might result in the reduction of liberty. "A new nation, conceived in liberty," would not wish, for the sake of unbroken civil peace, to debar legitimate efforts of free men to protest against injustices suffered or to probe toward the expansion or fuller realization of justice.

To insure domestic tranquility without encroaching upon liberties is a delicate assignment for the constitutional government of a free society. America's most penetrating nineteenth-century visitor, Tocqueville, wrote a warning on the point:

> The dread of disturbance and the love of well-being insensibly lead democratic nations to increase the functions of central government as the only power which appears to be intrinsically sufficently strong, enlightened, and secure to protect them from anarchy. . . . All the particular circumstances which tend to make the state of a democratic community agitated and precarious enhance the general propensity and lead private persons more and more to sacrifice their rights to their tranquility. . . . The love of *public tranquility* becomes . . . an indiscriminate passion, and the members of the community are apt to conceive a most inordinate devotion to order.

The point of the warning cannot be lost on the American people in our own day—a time of convulsive conflicts about social and racial injustice, about undeclared war, about the increasing incidence of crime and of random violence, about the bewildering speed of social change. We still have a fresh memory of actions taken in violation of laws to test their constitutionality. Only a short time ago mass protest meetings and parades took place, suggesting by their size and intensity the latent presence of violent disorder. New questions have been asked about the adequacy of existing means for effective civil dissent by lawful means, and about the proper understanding and role of civil disobedience. Something like a constitutional crisis arose from a line of decisions handed down, over bitter dissenting opinions, by the Warren Court in fourth, fifth, and sixth amendment cases—decisions that limited the power of police by affirming such procedural safeguards as enlarging prisoners' right to counsel and setting stricter standards for gathering evidence and conducting interrogations. A new administration and an altered Court have proceeded to a series of significant alterations in laws and in legal doctrine.

One thing remains constant. A constitutional government, charged "to insure domestic tranquility," must see to it that law enforcement is itself lawful, its processes articulated in law, its conduct subject to steady, critical, and politically accountable examination by the people.

. . . to . . . provide for the common defense, . . .

There can be no question of a general sort about the inclusion of this objective. Indeed Jay and Madison, in the *Federalist Papers*, spoke of it as "first":

> Among the many objects to which a wise and free people find it necessary to direct their attention, that of providing for their *safety* seems to be the first. The *safety* of the people 'doubtless has relation to a great variety of circumstances and considerations, and consequently affords great latitude to those who wish to define it precisely and comprehensively.
>
> At present I mean only to consider it as it respects security for the preservation of peace and tranquility, as well as against dangers from *foreign arms and influence,* as from dangers of the *like kind* arising from domestic causes. As the former of these comes first in order, it is proper it should be the first discussed. Let us therefore proceed to examine whether the people are not right in their opinion that a cordial Union, under an efficient national government, affords the best security that can be devised against *hostilities* from abroad [John Jay, *Federalist #3*].

> Security against foreign danger is one of the primitive objects of civil society. It is an avowed and essential object of the American Union. The powers requisite for attaining it must be effectually confided to the federal councils [James Madison, *Federalist #41*].

However, questions certainly did arise concerning how the defense would be "common," where and how the authority "to provide" for defense would be constitutionally placed, and how such authority could be limited so that its exercise would not threaten the concern for other objectives, especially the preservation of liberty. "The liberties of Rome," Madison wrote in *Federalist #41*, "proved the final victim to her military triumphs; . . . the liberties of Europe . . . have, with few exceptions, been the price of her military establishments."

In the consideration of such questions, certain premises were appealed to because of their clear relevance.

The Virginia Declaration of Rights, written by George Mason and adopted by the Virginia Constitutional Convention on June 12, 1776, was one of the central documents of the era. Section 13 of that Declaration read as follows:

> That a well-regulated militia, composed of the body of the people, trained to arms, is the proper, natural, and safe defense of a free state; that standing armies, in time of peace, should be avoided as dangerous to liberty; and that in all cases the military should be under strict subordination to, and governed by, the civil power.

The three propositions in that Section 13 probably circulated in the Grand Convention and in the ratifying conventions as propositions that should be regulative for the determination and ratification of the military part of the Constitution.

The first question concerned the placing of the authority for defense as between the states and the to-be-newly-constituted Federal Government. The Federal side of that argument was, of course, vigorously presented in the *Federalist Papers,* supporting the military sections of the proposed Constitution. In *Federalist #25,* Hamilton wrote:

> [The] transfer [of] the care of the common defense from the federal head to the individual members [would be] a project oppressive to some States, dangerous to all, and baneful to the Confederacy. . . . I expect we shall be told that the [States'] militia of the country is its natural bulwark, and would be at all times equal to the national defense. This doctrine, in substance, had like to have lost us our independence.

That moment of Hamiltonian scorn was not the best that he and Madison could do by way of persuasion. On behalf of the proposed Constitution's denial to the states of the right to raise armies, they spelled out again and again, in several of the *Federalist Papers,* the debilitating confusion that would arise from the opposite course, and the dire prospects of internecine warfare it could well bring. Indeed, of all the arguments for firm federal union probably the strongest was the argument that it was indispensable to providing for the common defense. In *Federalist #25,* Hamilton wrote: "The territories of Britain, Spain, and of the Indian nations in our neighborhood do not border on particular States, but encircle the Union from Maine to Georgia. The danger, though in different degrees, is therefore common. And the means of guarding against it ought, in like manner, to be the objects of the common councils and of a common treasury."

However, once granted that "the war power," as it later came to be called, should be predominantly placed in the national government (predominantly, because the state "militias" were constitutionally given a subordinate, counterbalancing role in national defense), the questions arose: How shall it be defined? How shall it be "limited," since, after all, constitutional government is limited government?

The apprehension in such questions was not taken lightly. Indeed, in *Federalist #8,* though he was there arguing for federal control of the war power, Hamilton spoke generally:

> Safety from external danger is the most powerful director of national conduct. Even the ardent love of liberty will, after a time, give way to its dictates. The violent destruction of life and property incident to war, the continual effort and alarm attendant on a state of continual danger, will compel nations the most attached to liberty to resort for repose and security to institutions which have a tendency to destroy their civil and political rights. To be more safe, they at length become willing to run the risk of being less free.

Immediately following that paragraph, the next paragraph begins: "The institutions chiefly alluded to are standing armies and the correspondent appendages of military establishments. Standing armies, it is said, are not provided against in the new Constitution; and it is therefore inferred that they may exist under it."

In fact, standing armies are not safeguarded against in the new Constitution. It is possible for them to exist under it. From six of the ratifying conventions came, in one form or another, amendments designed to keep faith with the national "prejudice" that standing peacetime armies are "ever a menace to liberty."

In countering that "prejudice" and defending the proposed Constitution, Madison and Hamilton did three things: First, they argued generally and, it would seem, convincingly that no restrictions could be rationally placed on the power to provide for the common defense; second, by tracing the historical origins of the "prejudice" against standing armies, they tried to show why it should not become immoderate: third, they argued prospectively that there was little likelihood that anything but a small standing army, no hazard to liberty, would ever be needed.

Two texts will suffice to delineate the argument against the irrationality of any restrictions on the power to provide for the common defense. In *Federalist* #23, Hamilton wrote as follows:

> The authorities essential to the common defense are these: to raise armies; to build and equip fleets; to prescribe rules for the government of both; to direct their operations; to provide for their support. These powers ought to exist without limitation, *because it is impossible to foresee or define the extent and variety of national exigencies, or the correspondent extent and variety of the means which may be necessary to satisfy them.* The circumstances that endanger the safety of nations are infinite, and for this reason no constitutional shackles can wisely be imposed on the power to which the care of it is committed. This power ought to be co-extensive with all the possible combinations of such circumstances. . . .
>
> This is one of those truths which, to a correct and unprejudiced mind, carries its own evidence along with it. . . . It rests upon [an] axiom as simple as [it is] universal; the *means* ought to be proportioned to the *end*.

In *Federalist* #41, Madison, noting that the issue had been confronted in earlier papers, nevertheless reiterated the argument:

> But was it necessary to give an indefinite power of raising troops, as well as providing fleets; and of maintaining both in peace, as well as in war? . . . The answer indeed seems to be so obvious and conclusive as scarcely to justify such a discussion in any place. With what color of propriety could the force necessary for defense be limited by those who cannot limit the force of offense? If a federal Constitution could chain the ambition or set bounds to the exertions of all other nations, then indeed might it prudently chain the discretion of its own government, and set bounds to the exertions for its own safety.
>
> How could a readiness for war in time of peace be safely prohibited, unless we could prohibit, in like manner, the preparations and establishments of every hostile nation? The means of security can only be regulated by the means and the danger of attack. They will, in fact, be ever determined by these rules, and by no others.

It is in vain to oppose constitutional barriers to the impulse of self-preservation.

Against the nearly axiomatic, "obvious," "conclusive" quality of such arguments for no restrictions, how could the "prejudice" against standing armies so stubbornly persist? Hamilton, in *Federalist* #26, proposed a genetic explanation. He wrote:

> The idea of restraining the legislative authority, in the means of providing for the national defense, is one of those refinements which owe their origin to a zeal for liberty more ardent than enlightened. . . . It may not be amiss in this place concisely to remark the origin and progress of the idea, which aims at the exclusion of military establishments in time of peace. Though in speculative minds it may arise from a contemplation of the nature and tendency of such institutions, fortified by the events that have happened in other ages and countries, yet as a national sentiment, it must be traced to those habits of thinking which we derive from the nation from whom the inhabitants of these States have in general sprung. [After a review of English constitutional history up to the 1689 Bill of Rights], the people of America may be said to have derived an hereditary impression of danger to liberty, from standing armies in time of peace. The circumstances of [the American] revolution quickened the public sensibility on every point connected with the security of popular rights, and in some instances raised the warmth of our zeal beyond the degree which consisted with the due temperature of the body politic. . . . The principles which had taught us to be jealous of the power of an hereditary monarch were by an injudicious excess extended to the representatives of the people in their popular assemblies.

In the last sentence, Hamilton was adverting to two facts: (1) that the article in the English Bill of Rights had read: "the raising or keeping a standing army within the kingdom in time of peace, unless with the consent of Parliament, was against law"; and (2) that in the proposed Constitution for the United States the power regarding standing armies resided in "the representatives of the people in their popular assemblies."

In the latter half of *Federalist* #26, and in other papers, Hamilton argued the extreme unlikelihood of "an army so large as seriously to menace the liberties of a great community." "What colorable reason could be assigned, in a country so situated, for such vast augmentations of the military force? It is impossible that the people would be long deceived; and the destruction of the project, and of the projectors, would quickly follow the discovery. . . . Upon what pretense could he [the Executive] be put in possession of a force of that magnitude in time of peace? . . . It is not easy to conceive a possibility that dangers so formidable can assail the whole Union as, to demand a force considerable enough to place our liberties in the least jeopardy." Before leaving this point, it should be noted that in tribute to the "prejudice" that regarded large standing armies as a danger to liberty, the actual practice in the subsequent century involved very small armies.

The direct address to the "prejudice" about standing armies was, however, only a part of the answer that could be given to expressions of dismay about the national government's being endowed with unlimited power in military affairs. The Framers, to restrain the domestic effects of the exercise of that power, resorted here, as in other dimensions of the Constitution, to the separation of powers and to the device of checks and balances.

For the purposes here, a concise summary is given in Walter Millis's 1959 pamphlet, *The Constitution and the Common Defense:*

> The President's exercise of his virtually absolute powers in the military and foreign field was controlled in the first instance by making him subject to impeachment and, quadrennially, to retirement by the electorate. His treaties were to be supreme law [and Jay in *Federalist #64* recognized, long before Senator Bricker, the possibility of "making law by treaty"], but this Executive invasion of the Legislative field was checked by requiring a two-thirds vote in the Senate for treaty ratification. There was no restriction upon his powers as commander-in-chief; but it was Congress which would raise, maintain, regulate, and provide the funds for the forces available to him to command. It was required that military, like other, appropriations must originate in the popular branch; and by restricting Army appropriations to run no more than two years, each new Congress was not only assured the opportunity but placed under the necessity of reviewing afresh the military establishment. The President's selection of military, as of other, officers was subject to Senatorial confirmation. Finally, the power to declare war was vested in the Congress, not the President.

Here, then, the Framers thought, was a powerful system of checks upon the exercise, by the President or the national government, of the almost absolute authority given them in the field of foreign and military policy. The *Federalist* authors argued for the adequacy of such checks as a protection to liberty. They adverted especially to the separation of the purse and the sword; to the two-year restriction on appropriations for the Army; and to the placing in Congress of the power to declare war. [When Pierce Butler, in the Convention, had wished to give that power to the President, Elbridge Gerry replied that he had "never expected to hear in a republic a motion to empower the Executive alone to declare war."]

However, the Constitution could not quite stop with such provisions for the assignment and the restraint of the war power. It had further to meet two of the deepest impulses of the times. Both were present in Section 13 of the Virginia Declaration of Rights, previously quoted. One was the reluctance of the states and state governments to surrender a complete monopoly of military power to the federal union. The other was the widespread conviction that only an armed people could remain a free people; the common defense, in the last analysis, could never be entrusted wholly to national armies but must remain in the hands of the people themselves.

The first concern was met in the ingenious compromises set forth in the clauses in Article I, Section VIII, that deal with the militia. The second concern was met by Madison's inclusion in his proposed Bill of Rights of what is now the Second Amendment.

Through the first seventy years of our history, the military establishment that issued from such provisions, checks, and compromises, in the opinion of Walter Millis, "operated with rather notable success to realize the hopes which had been pinned upon it." Millis goes on to say: "It averted inter-state or inter-sectional war by eliminating strategic and economic causes for one. Greatly aided, to be sure, by geography and the inter-national politics of the time, it relieved the young nation of the burdens and political perils of large standing armies. At the same time, it created a Union of sufficient military strength, actual or potential, to repel whatever military threats there were from the outside world." Neither the War of 1812 nor the Mexican War "led to any significant movement to revise the military structure or the military provisions of the Constitution."

It will serve the purpose here to continue to make use of Walter Millis's summary history of the fortunes of the military constitution.

His brief paragraph on the Civil War cannot help but produce a shudder about the misfortunes of human history:

> The Civil War, however, represented a cataclysmic failure of the military no less than of the political and economic compromises of the Constitution. *In a sense* the war was made possible only by that careful but, as it proved, unstable balance of Federal, state, and popular military power on which the Founders had insisted. It was Lincoln's call upon the militias of the border states to assist in suppressing their rebellious sister which forced the border to choose sides. It was the "preponderating influence" of the states over the militia, stressed by Hamilton, which had permitted the continued existence of at least partially trained and equipped state forces, owing their allegiance to the governors and legislatures rather than to the President and Congress, and so enabled the Southern states to rise. It was the absence of any large standing army which permitted the rising to reach the heights it did. The military guarantees which the Constitution had afforded the states proved to be real ones. To Southerners, the war vindicated the military no less than the political powers which had been left to the states precisely in order that they might repudiate a national "tyranny."

Millis continues: "But the South lost; and in the result the military balances of 1789 were destroyed or rendered meaningless."

There is no need for any attempt here at even a brief tracing of the steps from a military establishment comprising a small standing national army, state militias, and an armed citizenry, to the present colossal military establishment—huge in size and arsenal, globally stationed, biting deep into the budget, symbiotically related to a substantial part of the nation's industrial power and to scientific and technological research, raising issues of secrecy and using agencies of secret intelligence, and having immense impact not just on foreign policy but on domestic politics. Of course, this present military establishment has more than just the mission of "providing for the common defense," which was the only military mission for all but about the last thirty years of our nation's history; it also is judged necessary to support international commitments deemed to serve vital national interests and, in some interpretations, international interests as well.

It is therefore relevant to ask whether certain ingredients in "the American Testament" survive such a radical transformation in military size and missions. The question concerns not so much the constitutional devices as the fundamental judgments that led to their invention and adoption. In the last thirty years, during the era of confrontation and of major international commitments, the Framers' device of dual political control over the military has not worked very impressively. Before an increasing autocratic strain in the swollen Presidency and the strong positioning of the General Staff and its huge bureaucracy, Congress, perhaps, has appeared confused and more or less impotent. Until just recently, the purse was passed quickly to the sword. And Congress has acted as if it were embarrassed by its constitutional power "to declare war."

But what of the early national presuppositions that are parts of our testament? Do they hold as principles, however remote, on which to base judgments?

The Virginia Declaration of Rights affirmed that "in all cases the military should be under strict subordination to, and governed by, the civil power." No doubt a record of violations of the spirit, if not the letter, of that principle could be drawn up. A certain wariness on the point has not been absent. Yet, with all sorts of examples before us of military takeovers of governments and societies, it is often taken for granted that "it can't happen here."

Another proposition from the Virginia Declaration read: "Standing armies, in time of peace, are dangerous to liberty." In our time of precarious peace, we have a large standing army and multifarious military installations. Damages to liberty of the sort the Founders had in mind, from their memory of the Stuarts and of George III, have not occurred. But there are, perhaps, some indications that liberty is in jeopardy. Conscription and various kinds of job-dependencies in "defense industries" have engendered inroads on individual freedom. Civil liberties have not been firmly secure under recent governments that have been anxious about subversive beliefs, aroused mass protests, and collective actions of civil dissent. In general, political liberty is diminished in degree by the existence of a huge military establishment, because it is difficult for citizens to be constantly alert to its implications and consequences.

The Supreme Court, however, has developed a tradition of concern about threats to liberties from military establishments and aims. The Court's deliverances in this area, as in others, can be judged, in hindsight, as spotty. Certainly, one of the worst blemishes on its whole record was its endorsement of the treatment of West

Coast Japanese-American citizens at the outbreak of World War II. Yet, on the level of principle, there has been clarity. Two examples of judicial dicta are worth setting down here.

In a famous and major case involving the jurisdiction of military tribunals (*Ex parte Milligan,* 1866), Mr. Justice Davis, after declaring that the case "involves the very framework of the government and the fundamental principles of American liberty," and after reviewing the Constitutional provisions for liberties, wrote as follows:

> The Constitution of the United States is a law for rulers and people, equally in war and in peace, and covers with the shield of its protection all classes of men, at all times, and under all circumstances. No doctrine, involving more pernicious consequences, was ever invented by the wit of man than that any of its provisions can be suspended during any of the great exigencies of government.

In a 1948 case (*Woods* v. *Miller Co.*), Mr. Justice Jackson wrote as follows:

> The Government asserts no constitutional basis for this legislation other than this vague, undefined, and undefinable, "war power." *No one will question that this power is the most dangerous one to free government in the whole catalogue of powers.* It usually is invoked in haste and excitement when calm legislative consideration of constitutional limitation is difficult. It is executed in time of patriotic fervor that makes moderation unpopular. And, worst of all, it is interpreted by the Judges under the influence of the same passion and pressures. Always, as in this case, the Government urges hasty decision to forestall some emergency or serve some purpose and pleads that paralysis will result if its claims to power are denied or their confirmation delayed.
>
> Particularly when the war power is invoked to do things to the liberties of people, or to their property or economy that only indirectly affect conduct of the war and do not relate to the management of the war itself, the constitutional basis should be scrutinized with care.

By way of underlining a persistent continuity of thought on the subject, one can put with those two judicial texts (and there **are** many more) these words by Madison, "the father of the Constitution," who said in *Federalist #41:*

A standing force, therefore, is a dangerous, at the same time that it may be a necessary, provision. On the smallest scale it has its inconveniences. On an extensive scale its consequences may be fatal. On any scale it is an object of laudable circumspection and precaution. A wise nation will combine all these considerations; and, whilst it does not rashly preclude itself from any resource which may become essential to its safety, will exert all its prudence in diminishing both the necessity and the danger of resorting to one which may be inauspicious to its liberties.

... to ... promote the general welfare ...

The phrase "general welfare" had been present in the third article of the Articles of Confederation, which read: "The said states hereby severally enter into a firm league of friendship with each other, for their common defense, the security of their liberties, and their mutual and general welfare." It is in no way clear what the phrase there meant. If it was interpreted as equivalent to "the common good," "the public good," "the common weal," or "general happiness," it would then be designating the all-embracing comprehensive end of government. With so broad a meaning, it could not logically be placed in the Preamble to the Constitution as one of six purposes that together constitute an articulation of the complex structure of the common good, with which it was identical.

The phrase gained its specific meaning, not from any early elucidation of the Preamble, but rather from discussion during the period of ratification and from later constitutional developments occasioned by the occurrence of the same phrase in the taxing clause of the Constitution. The first paragraph of Article I, Section 8, reads: "The Congress shall have power to lay and collect taxes, duties, imposts, and excises, to pay the debts and provide for the common defense and general welfare of the United States." There then follows an enumeration of specific things that Congress is empowered to do, first, an odd assortment of fiscal and military things, and then an odd assortment of things neither fiscal nor military. Section 8 ends with what came to be called "the sweeping clause": "The Congress shall have power ... to make all laws which shall be necessary and proper for carrying into execution the foregoing powers and all other powers vested by this Constitution in the government of the United States, or in any department or officer thereof."

Power to tax and spend for "the general welfare," with the additional provision of "power to make all laws which shall be necessary and proper for carrying into execution the foregoing powers" —that sounds like very great power, indeed! Madison, in *Federalist #41*, took note of a fierce attack on the language of the first paragraph of Article I, Section 8, on the ground that it would amount "to an unlimited commission to exercise every power which may be alleged to be necessary for the common defense or general welfare." He undertook to ward off such an attack by saying that the first paragraph did not announce a separate power to tax and spend for the general welfare; that it was just an introductory heading for the powers specified in the following paragraphs of Section 8; that the taxing-and-spending power was limited to those specified powers. With that interpretation, Madison was not merely pleading for ratification. He fervently believed, and continued to believe, along with Jefferson in their later opposition to Hamilton, that the major issue of limited versus unlimited government was at stake in the interpretation placed on the reference to general welfare in the first paragraph of Article I, Section 8.

Madison may have been right about the original intentions behind the phrase "general welfare" in that Section. He was, after all, "the father of the Constitution." But the matter was not put to rest by his vehement words on the subject in *Federalist #41*.

In December of 1791, Hamilton, the Secretary of the Treasury, presented to Congress his bold and brilliant *Report on Manufactures*. He worked into that document his own constitutional interpretation:

A question has been made concerning the constitutional right of the Government of the United States to apply this species of encouragement, but there is certainly no good foundation for such a question. The National Legislature has express authority "to lay and collect taxes . . . and provide for the . . . general welfare." . . . These three qualifications excepted, the power to *raise money* is *plenary* and *indefinite*. . . . The phrase [general welfare] is as comprehensive as any that could have been used, because it was not fit that the constitutional authority of the Union to appropriate its revenues should have been restricted within narrower limits than the "general welfare," and because this necessarily embraces a vast variety of particulars, which are susceptible neither of specification nor of definition.

It is, therefore, of necessity, left to the discretion of the National Legislature to pronounce upon the objects, which concern the general welfare, and for which, under that description, an appropriation of money is requisite and proper.

Jefferson spoke of this privately to Washington, urging that Hamilton's proposition seemed to go "far beyond every one ever yet advanced" toward making the Constitution "a very different thing from what the people thought they had submitted to," and had indeed forced the people to consider "whether we live under a limited or an unlimited government." Madison wrote to the Governor of Virginia: "What think you of the [Hamilton's] commentary . . . on the term 'general welfare'? The federal government has been hitherto limited to the specified powers, by the Greatest Champions for Latitude in expounding those powers—If not only the means, but the objects are unlimited, the parchment had better be thrown into the fire at once." On the floor of the House, Madison repeated his view that the words "general welfare" were simply "a sort of caption or general description of the specific powers" that followed, and had "no further meaning" and gave no "further power" than what could be "found in that specification." "In short, sir," Madison concluded,

. . . I venture to declare it as my opinion that were the power of Congress to be established in the latitude contended for, it would subvert the very foundation and transmute the very nature of the limited government established by the people of America; and what inferences might be drawn, or what consequences ensue from such a step, it is incumbent on us all well to consider.

Madison was persuasive in the House. Hamilton suffered a major defeat. His important *Report on Manufactures* was pigeonholed.

The argument, however, was far from over. Although one or another sort of welfare legislation did get passed, the constitutional issue was not raised until well into the twentieth century. It was the Great Depression that brought the Supreme Court, in a series of cases during 1936–37, to resolve, in Hamilton's favor, his dispute with Madison about the range of the power of Congress "to promote the general welfare."

In the case of *United States* v. *Butler* (1936), in which, for a side reason, the decision went against the Agricultural Adjustment

Act (involving subsidies for reduction of the farm surplus), Mr. Justice Roberts's opinion for the court reviewed the doctrinal quarrel and explicitly settled it in Hamilton's favor:

> The argument is that Congress may appropriate and authorize the spending of moneys for the "general welfare"; that the phrase should be liberally construed to cover anything conducive to national welfare. . . .
>
> Since the foundation of the nation sharp differences of opinion have persisted as to the true interpretation of the phrase. Madison asserted it amounted to no more than a reference to the other powers enumerated in the subsequent clauses of the same section; that, as the United States is a government of limited and enumerated powers, the grant of the power to tax and spend for the general national welfare must be confined to the enumerated legislative fields committed to the Congress. . . . Hamilton, on the other hand, maintained the clause confers a power separate and distinct from those later enumerated, is not restricted in meaning by the grant of them, and Congress consequently has a substantive power to tax and to appropriate, limited only by the requirement that it shall be exercised to provide for the general [not local] welfare of the United States.
>
> Each contention has had the support of those whose views are entitled to weight. This Court has noticed the question, but has never found it necessary to decide which is the true construction. Mr. Justice Story, in his Commentaries, espouses the Hamiltonian position. We shall not review the writing of public men and commentators or discuss the legislative practice. Study of all these leads us to conclude that the reading advocated by Mr. Justice Story is the correct one. While, therefore, the power to tax is not unlimited, its confines are set in the clause which confers it, and not in those of Section 8 which bestow and define the legislative powers of the Congress. It results that the power of Congress to authorize expenditure of public moneys for public purposes is not limited by the direct grants of legislative power found in the Constitution.

Two immediately ensuing cases in 1937 are also worth noting. They are concerned with the constitutionality of different Titles in the Social Security Act of 1935. In both cases, that act is upheld in the decision. In both cases, the opinion for the Court was delivered by Mr. Justice Cardozo. In both cases, he adverted to the doctrine in *United States* v. *Butler,* set forth just above.

The first case, *Steward Machine Co.* v. *Davis* (1937), involved

Title III of the Social Security Act, which authorized appropriations from the general revenue funds for the purpose of assisting the states in the administration of their *unemployment compensation* laws. Cardozo wrote:

> During the years 1929 to 1936, when the country was passing through a cyclical depression, the number of the unemployed mounted to unprecedented heights. Often the average was more than 10 million; at times a peak was attained of 16 million or more. Disaster to the breadwinner meant disaster to dependents. Accordingly the roll of the unemployed, itself formidable enough, was only a partial roll of the destitute or needy. The fact developed quickly that the states were unable to give the requisite relief. The problem had become national in area and dimensions. There was need of help from the nation if the people were not to starve. It is too late today for the argument to be heard with tolerance that in a crisis so extreme the use of the moneys of the nation to relieve the unemployed and their dependents is a use for any purpose narrower than the promotion of the general welfare. CF. *United States* v. *Butler;* and *Helvering* v. *Davis* decided herewith.

In a companion case to *Steward,* the case of *Helvering* v. *Davis* (1937), the Court sustained the old age pensions provisions of the Social Security Act (Titles II and VIII), which imposed taxes on employers and employees and authorized appropriations to pay old age pensions to eligible previous employees in an exclusively federal program. Cardozo wrote:

> The purge of nation-wide calamity that began in 1929 has taught us many lessons. Not the least is the solidarity of interests that may once have seemed to be divided. . . . Spreading from state to state, unemployment is an ill not particular but general, which may be checked, if Congress so determines, by the resources of the nation. If this can have been doubtful until now, our ruling today in the case of the Steward Machine Co., has set the doubt at rest.
>
> But the ill is all one or at least not greatly different whether men are thrown out of work because there is no longer work to do or because the disabilities of age make them incapable of doing it. Rescue becomes necessary irrespective of the cause. The hope behind this statute is to save men and women from the rigors of the poor house as well as from the haunting fear that such a lot awaits them when journey's end is near.

Within seven years, the idea of "the general welfare" implicit in such cases received an exuberant expansion. President Roosevelt's State of the Union message on January 11, 1944, first dealt with measures needed to continue the prosecution of the war with vigor. He closed with a vision of how the peace should be prosecuted:

It is our duty now to begin to lay the plans and determine the strategy for the winning of a lasting peace and the establishing of an American standard of living higher than ever before known. We cannot be content, no matter how high that general standard of living may be, if some fraction of our people—whether it be one-third or one-fifth or one-tenth—is ill-fed, ill-clothed, ill-housed, and insecure.

This republic had its beginning, and grew to its present strength, under the protection of certain inalienable political rights—among them the right of free speech, free press, free worship, trial by jury, freedom from unreasonable searches and seizures. They were our rights to life and liberty. As our nation has grown in size and stature, however—as our industrial economy expanded—these political rights proved inadequate to assure us equality in the pursuit of happiness.

We have come to a clear realization of the fact that true individual freedom cannot exist without economic security and independence. "Necessitous men are not freemen." People who are hungry and out of a job are the stuff of which dictatorships are made. In our day these economic truths have become accepted as self-evident. We have accepted, so to speak, a second Bill of Rights under which a new basis of security and prosperity can be established for all—regardless of station, race, or creed.

Among these are:

The right to a useful and remunerative job in the industries or shops or farms or mines of the nation;

The right to earn enough to provide adequate food and clothing and recreation;

The right of every farmer to raise and sell his products at a return which will give him and his family a decent living;

The right of every businessman, large and small, to trade in an atmosphere of freedom from unfair competition and domination by monopolies at home or abroad;

The right of every family to a decent home;

The right to adequate medical care and the opportunity to achieve and enjoy good health;

The right to adequate protection from the economic fears of old
age, sickness, accident, and unemployment;

The right to a good education.

All of these rights spell security. And after this war is won, we
must be prepared to move forward, in the implementation of these
rights, to new goals of human happiness and well-being. America's
own rightful place in the world depends in large part upon how
fully these and similar rights have been carried into practice for
our citizens. For unless there is security here at home there cannot
be lasting peace in the world. . . .

I ask the Congress to explore the means for implementing this
economic bill of rights—for it is definitely the responsibility of the
Congress so to do.

That 1944 State of the Union message was delivered at some
considerable temporal distance from the Declaration of Independence, from the Preamble's statement of the promotion of the general welfare as one of the objectives of government, and from the
dispute between Founding Fathers about the power of Congress
to promote the general welfare.

However, it is clear that Roosevelt's impassioned proclamation
draws its inspiration, its terms of discourse, indeed its very diction,
from Jefferson's Declaration of Independence. It is likewise clear
that Roosevelt's boldness about what "it is definitely the responsibility of the Congress so to do" derives from the Depression Court's
decisions that Hamilton was right about the plenary power that
Congress has, under the Constitution, to promote the general welfare.

Roosevelt did not use the term "general welfare." He mentioned
"new goals of human happiness and well-being." He clearly sub-
sumed "the welfare power," to call it that by analogy to "the war
power," under the Declaration of Independence's assertion that an
overriding objective of government was to secure—that is, make
secure—the natural right to the pursuit of happiness.

He called his second bill of rights a bill of economic rights. The
term "economic" is used very broadly. It is worth remembering that
Hamilton's interpretation of the Constitution, in his *Report on
Manufactures,* did not occur in a context of an emergency concern
for the desperate plight of unfortunate citizens suffering from a
depression. Hamilton wanted Congress to promote the general wel-

fare by assistance to the growth of businesses. All governmental actions in aid of "the economy," to fight inflation or recession, would be as much exercises of the welfare power as measures of assistance to the seriously indigent, the debilitated old, the helplessly sick or disabled, and those whom we have the habit of speaking of as "on welfare." Roosevelt's very broad use of the term "economic" includes such things as the right to a decent home, the right to adequate medical care, the right to sufficient schooling, as well as the rights of every farmer and every businessman. Used thus broadly, the term encompasses all the external conditions which can be judged indispensable to leading a decent human life.

Roosevelt explicitly declared that the promotion of the general economic welfare and the implementation of specifically economic rights were necessary if "true individual freedom" is to thrive. More than that, such measures are indispensable if the pursuit of happiness by every human being is to be more than an ineffectual right. The participation by every human being in the general economic welfare and the recognition of his basic economic rights provide him with the enabling means or facilitating conditions without which he must inevitably be impeded if not totally frustrated in his effort to pursue happiness—to make a good life for himself.

A government cannot guarantee to all the attainment of happiness; it cannot even provide them with all the conditions that they need for a modicum of success in the effort to live humanly well, such as moral virtue and the gifts of good fortune; but the one thing it can do, and do effectively, is to provide human beings with the external conditions they need in order to lead decent human lives—economic goods or benefits of all sorts in addition to civil peace, political liberty, and a just social order.

The whole of Roosevelt's State of the Union Address in 1944 charges Congress with the task of doing distributive justice. To assure to all "equality in the pursuit of happiness" is a work of justice. All human beings, equally in possession of the inherent human right to pursue happiness, can rightfully expect from the political society of which they are members and from the government of which they are together constituents, proportionately equitable support in their exercise of that right. Justice requires government to promote the general welfare, understood as an equitable participation by all in the economic or other external goods which are judged indispensable to the pursuit of happiness.

All human beings should have an equal opportunity to fare well in that pursuit.

> . . . and secure the blessings of liberty to ourselves
> and our posterity, . . .

Closing his lectures on *Constitutionalism: Ancient and Modern,* Charles H. McIlwain wrote: "The two fundamental correlative elements of constitutionalism for which all lovers of liberty must yet fight are the legal limits to artbitrary power and a complete political responsibility of government to the governed."

That sentence, written in 1940, could have been uttered in an opening address to the Constitutional Convention in Philadelphia in 1787. Americans had proved themselves "lovers of liberty" in their resistance to arbitrary British power and in their war for independence. They were to consummate their revolution by "ordaining and establishing a Constitution for the United States of America." On the Fourth of July, 1788, James Wilson delivered an oration, at the procession formed at Philadelphia, to celebrate the adoption of the Constitution of the United States. In his proem, Wilson said:

> A people free and enlightened, establishing and ratifying a system of government, which they have previously considered, examined, and approved! This is the spectacle, which we are assembled to celebrate; and it is the most dignified one that has yet appeared on our globe. . . . What is the object exhibited to our contemplation? A whole people exercising its first and greatest power—performing an act of sovereignty, original and unlimited!

In an only slightly less exclamatory way, Madison was to write in 1792:

> In Europe, charters of liberty have been granted by power. America has set the example and France has followed it, of charters of power granted by liberty. This revolution in the practice of the world may, with an honest praise, be pronounced the most triumphant epoch of its history and the most consoling presage of its happiness.

A free and enlightened people performing an act of sovereignty, original and unlimited! A charter of power granted by liberty!

These exclamations were after the fact. In the actual work of ordaining a new Constitution, the Framers were anything but naïve about arbitrary power. Indeed, when they had been British subjects, the Americans were fervently proud of their British liberties. They had by no means forgotten the victories over arbitrary power by which the liberties of Englishmen had been secured. They knew and prized the documents that recorded those victories, documents comprised by what the elder Pitt called "the Bible of the English Constitution"—Magna Carta, the Petition of Right, and the Bill of Rights after the Glorious Revolution of 1688.

Indeed, it was precisely because they remembered those documents, as well as recent royal and parliamentary acts of arbitrary power, that the Framers proceeded, as "lovers of liberty," to place legal limits on the charter of power they were about to grant. In so doing, they borrowed heavily, often in direct wording, from "the Bible of the English Constitution."

In *Federalist #51*, Madison stated the Framers' concern for the first element of constitutionalism:

> If men were angels, no government would be necessary. If angels were to govern men, neither external nor internal controls on government would be necessary. In framing a government which is to be administered by men over men, the great difficulty lies in this: you must first enable the government to control the governed; and in the next place oblige it to control itself. A dependence on the people is, no doubt, the primary control on the government; but experience has taught mankind the necessity of auxiliary precautions.

In the context of *Federalist #51*, Madison was pondering the task of laying "a due foundation for that separate and distinct exercise of the different powers of government, which to a certain extent is admitted on all hands to be essential to the preservation of liberty."

However, in addition to the broad ideas about the precautions that might be effected by the separation of powers and by checks and balances, the Constitution of 1787 contains a composite of many mutually reinforcing guarantees of individual rights, and of limitations on federal and state governments. The Constitution in its main body forbids suspension of the writ of habeas corpus except in cases of rebellion or invasion; prohibits state or federal bills of attainder and ex post facto laws; requires that all crimes against the United States be tried by jury in the state where committed; limits the definition, trial, and punishment of treason; prohibits titles of nobility and religious tests for officeholding; guarantees a republican form of government in every state; and assures each citizen of the privileges and immunities of the citizens of the several states.

Popular dissatisfaction with the inadequacy of the guarantees in the main body of the Constitution, which was repeatedly expressed in the state ratifying conventions, led to firm demands and consequent promises, which eventuated in the first ten amendments. These amendments have always been regarded as a Bill of Rights. That term, however, should be extended to include not only the limitations in the main body of the Constitution, but also those in later amendments—those that abolish slavery; declare all persons born or naturalized in the United States and subject to its jurisdiction as citizens thereof; forbid the states to abridge the privileges or immunities of citizens of the United States, to deprive any person of life, liberty, or property without due process of law, or to deny to any person the equal protection of the laws; prohibit the denial or abridgment of voting rights because of race, sex, or failure to pay poll taxes.

By such an extended Bill of Rights, taken together with the results of the separation of powers and of checks and balances, Americans placed constitutional limits on arbitrary power. These constitutional limitations intended to provide basic security for one freedom, fundamental throughout the revolutionary era—freedom *from* arbitrary power. The revolutionary Americans had freed themselves from British arbitrary power. Their posterity should not be exposed to arbitrary power exercised by the government the Founding Fathers were here ordaining.

The second of McIlwain's "two fundamental correlative elements of constitutionalism" is "a complete political responsibility of government to the governed." Constitutional arrangements to satisfy such an ideal would make the new nation a republic—a self-ruling people.

Madison's definition of a "republic" in *Federalist* #10 was succinct enough: "A republic, by which I mean a government in which the scheme of representation takes place." Another, fuller, and famous passage, in *Federalist* #39, connects the term "republic" with "self-government": "The first question that offers itself is, whether the general form and aspect of the government be strictly republican. It is evident that no other form would be reconcilable with the genius of the people of America; with the fundamental principles of the Revolution; or with that honorable determination which animates every votary of freedom, to rest all our political experiments on the capacity of mankind for self-government." The people of a republic, with a government in which some system of representation is operative, is a self-governing people.

Such a high claim puts a heavy burden on what has certainly come to be considered an elusive and complicated idea—the idea of representation. Indeed, the revolutionary period had its beginning in a dispute revolving around that idea. Bernard Bailyn writes: "The question of representation was the first serious intellectual problem to come between England and the colonies, and while it was not the most important issue involved in the Anglo-American controversy (the whole matter of taxation and representation was 'a mere incident,' McIlwain has observed, in a much more basic constitutional struggle), it received the earliest and most exhaustive examination and underwent a most revealing transformation." The history of that transformation is complicated, but its direction is clear.

Edmund Burke's idea of "virtual representation" (by unelected representatives) was ridiculed by Daniel Dulany in a powerful pamphlet, *Considerations on the Propriety of Imposing Taxes in the British Colonies, for the Purpose of Raising a Revenue, by Act of Parliament.* Representation had to stem from electoral power in the citizens, and that would extend to measures for choosing the first elected chief executive the world had ever seen.

More important, the leaders in the early revolutionary period rejected Burke's theory of representation, which he had expressed in words now famous: "Parliament is not a congress of ambassadors from different and hostile interests; which interests each must maintain, as an agent and advocate, against other agents and advocates; but Parliament is a deliberative assembly of one nation, with one interest, that of the whole; where, not local purposes, not local prejudices ought to guide, but the general good, resulting from the general reason of the whole." The contrary doctrine, to which the Americans appealed, was precisely one that declared "representatives" to be "agents and advocates," to whom "instructions" could be given. In 1774, James Wilson, America's leading jurist, wrote, "The interest of the representatives is the same with that of their constituents," and again, "representatives are reminded [by electoral acts] whose creatures they are; and to whom they are accountable for the use of that power, which is delegated unto them." Section 2 of the 1776 Virginia Declaration of Rights read: "That all power is vested in, and consequently derived from, the people; that magistrates are their trustees and servants and at all times amenable [accountable] to them." The records of the Convention of 1787 show James Wilson as having said: "The Legislature ought to be the most exact transcript of the whole Society. Representation is made necessary only because it is impossible for the people to act collectively." On a later occasion, he also said that: "The Doctrine of Representation is this—first, the representative ought to speak the Language of his Constituents, and secondly, that his language or vote should have the same influence as though the Constituents gave it." This tendency is summed up in a letter written by Thomas Jefferson in 1816, altering Madison's definition of a republic: "Were I to assign to this term a precise and definite idea, I would say that, purely and simply, [the term "republic"] means a government by its citizens in mass, acting directly and personally according to rules established by the majority; and that every other government is more or less republican, in proportion as it has in its composition more or less of this ingredient of the direct action of the citizens."

The conviction was so strong about the doctrine of instructions— the doctrine that at any time a clear expression of the will of the majority of constituents is binding on the action of their representative—that some of the new state constitutions, after independence, provided for it. However, in the First Congress, a proposal to include the right to instruct representatives in the Bill of Rights was voted down by a large majority. Questions had begun to arise about what a sound theory of representation might entail.

The last word here, on representation and elections, can come from James Wilson, lecturing on law in the College of Philadelphia after his term as member of the first Supreme Court. His words steer clear of hard questions about the idea of representation and emphasize the need for more experience with elections and with the representative bodies they select:

Of the science of just and equal government, the progress, as we have formerly seen, has been small and slow. Peculiarly small and slow has it been, in the discovery and improvement of the interesting doctrines of election and representation. If, with regard to other subjects, government may be said, as it has been said, to be still in its infancy; we may, with regard to this subject, consider it as only in its childhood. And yet this is the subject, which must form the basis of every government, that is, at once, efficient, respectable, and free.

The pyramid of government—and a republican government may well receive that beautiful and solid form—should be raised to a dignified altitude: but its foundations must, of consequence, be broad, and strong, and deep. The authority, the interests, and the affections of the people at large are the only foundation, on which a superstructure, proposed to be at once durable and magnificent, can be rationally erected.

Representation is the chain of communication between the people and those, to whom they have committed the exercise of the powers of government. If the materials, which form this chain, are sound and strong, it is unnecessary to be solicitous about the very high degree to which they are polished. But in order to impart to them the true republican luster, I know no means more effectual than to invite and admit the freemen to the right of suffrage, and to enhance, as much as possible, the value of that right. Its value cannot, in truth, be enhanced too highly. It is a right of the greatest import, and of the most improving efficacy. It is a right to choose those, who shall be intrusted with the authority and with the confidence of the people: and who may employ that authority and that confidence for the noblest interests of the commonwealth, wtihout the apprehension of disappointment or control.

This surely must have a powerful tendency to open, to enlighten, to enlarge, and to exalt the mind. I cannot, with sufficient energy, express my own conceptions of the value and the dignity of this right. In real majesty, an independent and unbiased elector stands superior to princes, addressed by the proudest titles, attended by the most magnificent retinues, and decorated with the most splendid ragalia. Their sovereignty is only derivative, like the pale light of the moon: his is original, like the beaming splendor of the sun.

The benign influences, flowing from the possession and exercise of this right, deserve to be clearly and fully pointed out. I wish it was in my power to do complete justice to the important

subject. Hitherto those benign influences have been little understood; they have been less valued; they have been still less experi-
enced. This part of the knowledge and practice of government is
yet, as has been observed, in its childhood. Let us, however, nurse
and nourish it. In due time, it will repay our care and our labor;
for, in due time, it will grow to the strength and stature of a full
and perfect man.

One further point remains to be made—the point that the "two
fundamental elements of constitutionalism" are, indeed, "correlative." A whole range of civil liberties, involving legal limitations
on the powers of government, are precisely the liberties by which
the people are assured security for their development and exercise
of electoral judgment, and for holding their government at all
times accountable.

The point is amply clear insofar as it touches the political meaning of all the First Amendment rights. In addition to those rights
are the civil liberties indispensable to safeguarding the people's
position as the standing principal ruler, such as protection from
arbitrary arrest and imprisonment, from bills of attainder often used
in the past to silence political opposition, from unreasonable and
arbitrary searches and seizures.

There can be no doubt that the main preoccupation during the
Revolutionary and the Constitution-making periods was with
political liberty—in its two dimensions, one involving a freedom
from arbitrary power, the other involving freedoms for the task of
keeping government accountable for its performance within the
powers assigned to it.

The general criterion for judgments of governmental performance *intra vires* involved another liberty, which can appropriately
be designated personal liberty. Indeed, personal liberty was more
fundamental than the two aforementioned political liberties, since
they, in effect, served to protect it. In significant measure, personal
liberty was grounded in law, in the sense of being "secured" by law
and government.

How would such personal liberty have been defined by the
American founding leaders? In the context of the Declaration of
Independence, personal liberty would consist in the capacity to
exercise effectively the natural right equally possessed by all men
to the pursuit of happiness. Was government necessary for confer-

ring such liberty on citizens and safeguarding it? The answer was firmly in the affirmative. Are not laws antithetical to such liberty, so that the more law, the less liberty? The answer was firmly in the negative.

All the leaders of the founding generation were well acquainted with John Locke's *Second Treatise on Civil Government*. There is no evidence anywhere that there was any fundamental disagreement with his "resolution" of age-old questions about the relation between law and liberty.

In Chapter IV of his treatise, a chapter interestingly enough entitled "Of Slavery," Locke wrote as follows:

> The natural liberty of man is to be free from any superior power on earth, and not to be under the will or legislative authority of man, but to have only the law of Nature for his rule. The liberty of man in society is to be under no other legislative power but that established by consent in the commonwealth, nor under the dominion of any will, or restraint of any law, but what that legislative shall enact according to the trust put in it. Freedom, then, is not what Sir Robert Filmer tells us: "A liberty for every one to do what he lists, to live as he pleases, and not to be tied by any laws"; but freedom of men under government is to have a standing rule to live by, common to every one of that society, and made by the legislative power erected in it. A liberty to follow my own will in all things where that rule prescribes not, not to be subject to the inconstant, uncertain, unknown, arbitrary will of another man, as freedom of nature is to be under no other restraint but the law of Nature.
>
> This freedom from absolute, arbitrary power is so necessary to, and closely joined with, a man's preservation, that he cannot part with it but by what forfeits his preservation and life together.

The same points are somewhat more amply stated in Locke's Chapter VI:

> For law, in its true notion, is not so much the limitation as the direction of a free and intelligent agent to his proper interest, and prescribes no farther than is for the general good of those under that law. Could they be happier without it, the law, as a useless thing, would of itself vanish; and that ill deserves the name of confinement which hedges us in only from bogs and precipices. So that however it may be mistaken, the end of law is not to

abolish or restrain, but to preserve and enlarge freedom. For in all the states of created beings, capable of laws, where there is no law there is no freedom. For liberty is to be free from restraint and violence from others, which cannot be where there is no law; and is not, as we are told, "a liberty for every man to do what he lists." For who could be free, when every other man's humor might domineer over him? But a liberty to dispose and order freely as he lists his person, actions, possessions, and his whole property within the allowance of those laws under which he is, and therein not to be subject to the arbitrary will of another, but freely follow his own.

It is important, perhaps, to look once more at that part of the first text quoted from Locke where, after speaking of freedom under law, he refers to a sphere of freedom in which every one has "a liberty to follow [his] own will in all things where that rule prescribes not." Whatever may have been Locke's views concerning the desirable scope of that sphere in which laws do not regulate human conduct and individuals are free to do as they please, it is worth recording that there is no body of texts in the founding literature which urges that the sphere of unregulated conduct should be very large, or as large as possible. That literature, in other words, does not espouse the position later to be called "minimalism" —the view that that government governs best which governs least, because it thereby enlarges the sphere of personal liberty. It was left open to future history to determine how much legal regulation is needed to secure, indeed to preserve and enlarge, personal liberty.

For final confirmation of the American consensus on Locke's theory of the relation of law and liberty, a text from James Wilson serves best. It not only confirms Locke's doctrine, but also argues, by implication at least, that that government governs best which governs, not least or most, but most justly; and that human beings have as much personal liberty as they deserve, or can use justly, when their conduct is regulated by just laws. The passage from James Wilson reads as follows:

In a former part of these lectures, I had occasion to describe what natural liberty is: let us recur to the description, which was then given. "Nature has implanted in man the desire of his own happiness; she has inspired him with many tender affections towards others, especially in the near relations of life; she has endowed him with intellectual and with active powers; she has furnished him with a natural impulse to exercise his powers for his own happiness, and the happiness of those for whom he entertains such tender affections. If all this be true, the undeniable consequence is, that he has a right to exert those powers for the accomplishment of those purposes, in such a manner, and upon such objects, as his inclination and judgment shall direct; provided he does no injury to others; and provided some public interests do not demand his labors. This right is natural liberty."

If this description of natural liberty is a just one, it will teach us, that selfishness and injury are as little countenanced by the law of nature as by the law of man. Positive penalties, indeed, may, by human laws, be annexed to both. But these penalties are a restraint only upon injustice and overweening self-love, not upon the exercise of natural liberty.

In a state of natural liberty, every one is allowed to act according to his own inclination, provided he transgress not those limits, which are assigned to him by the law of nature: in a state of civil liberty, he is allowed to act according to his inclination, provided he transgress not those limits, which are assigned to him by the municipal law. True it is, that, by the municipal law, some things may be prohibited, which are not prohibited by the law of nature: but equally true it is, that, under a government which is wise and good, every citizen will gain more liberty than he can lose by these prohibitions. He will gain more by the limitation of other men's freedom, than he can lose by the diminution of his own. He will gain more by the enlarged and undisturbed exercise of his natural liberty in innumerable instances, than he can lose by the restriction of it in a few.

Upon the whole, therefore, man's natural liberty, instead of being abridged, may be increased and secured in a government, which is good and wise. As it is with regard to his natural liberty, so it is with regard to his other natural rights.

The title page of the first published edition of James Wilson's *Works* contained a motto from Cicero: Lex fundamentum est libertatis, qua fruimur. Legum omnes servi sumus, ut liberi esse possimus. "Law is the foundation of the liberty we enjoy. We are all servants of the laws in order that we can be free."

The Gettysburg Address

FOUR SCORE AND SEVEN YEARS AGO our fathers brought forth on this continent a new nation, conceived in liberty and dedicated to the proposition that all men are created equal.

Now we are engaged in a great civil war, testing whether that nation or any nation so conceived and so dedicated can long endure. We are met on a great battlefield of that war. We have come to dedicate a portion of that field as a final resting place for those who here gave their lives that that nation might live. It is altogether fitting and proper that we should do this.

But, in a larger sense, we cannot dedicate—we cannot consecrate—we cannot hallow—this ground. The brave men, living and dead, who struggled here have consecrated it far above our poor power to add or detract. The world will little note nor long remember what we say here, but it can never forget what they did here. It is for us, the living, rather, to be dedicated here to the unfinished work which they who fought here have thus far so nobly advanced.

It is rather for us to be here dedicated to the great task remaining before us—that from these honored dead we take increased devotion to that cause for which they gave the last full measure of devotion, that we here highly resolve that these dead shall not have died in vain, that this nation, under God, shall have a new birth of freedom; and that government of the people, by the people, for the people shall not perish from the earth.

The Gettysburg Address

ONE of the ceremonies arranged by the United States Civil War Centennial Commission commemorated the Gettysburg Address. At that ceremony, the poet Robert Lowell said: "The Gettysburg Address is a symbolic and sacramental act. Its verbal quality is resonance combined with a logical, matter of fact, prosaic brevity."

The main intent here is to comment on the last clause of the Address, with its famous triad of prepositional phrases. However, the "resonance" Lowell spoke of should be briefly noted. That resonance, occurring on a "great battlefield" in "a great civil war," gives the Address its testamentary quality and grounds the plea for a renewed dedication.

> **Four score and seven years ago our fathers brought forth on this continent a new nation, . . .**

That the nation's birth date is July 4, 1776, is something we cannot imagine as ever having been in dispute. But it was not something taken for granted by Lincoln nor perfunctory for him. In his years of argument against the extension of slavery to new territories, Lincoln repeatedly appealed to the Declaration of Independence. His opponents resorted to the Constitution, with its covert references to the institution of slavery, as decisive for issues of policy regarding the extension of slavery. In effect, they took the adoption of the Constitution as the juridical birth date of the nation.

The impromptu remarks Lincoln made in Independence Hall, Philadelphia, February 22, 1861, on the eve of his inauguration, expressed his conviction about the guiding power of the Declaration of Independence.[1]

I am filled with deep emotion at finding myself standing here in the place where were collected together the wisdom, the patriotism, the devotion to principle, from which sprang the institutions under which we live. You have kindly suggested to me that in my hands is the task of restoring peace to our distracted country. I can say in return, sir, that all the political sentiments I entertain have been drawn, so far as I have been able to draw them, from the sentiments which originated, and were given to the world from this hall in which we stand. I have never had a feeling politically that did not spring from the sentiments embodied in the Declaration of Independence. I have often pondered over the dangers which were incurred by the men who assembled here and adopted that Declaration of Independence—I have pondered over the toils that were endured by the officers and soldiers of the army, who achieved that Independence. I have often inquired of myself, what great principle or idea it was that kept this Confederacy so long together. It was not the mere matter of the separation of the colonies from the mother land; but something in that Declaration giving liberty, not alone to the people of this country, but hope to the world for all future time. It was that which gave promise that in due time the weights should be lifted from the shoulders of all men, and that *all* should have an equal chance. This is the sentiment embodied in that Declaration of Independence.

Now, my friends, can this country be saved upon that basis? If it can, I will consider myself one of the happiest men in the world if I can help to save it. If it can't be saved upon that principle, it will be truly awful. But, if this country cannot be saved without giving up that principle—I was about to say I would rather be assassinated on this spot than to surrender it.

[1] A small anthology of Lincoln's appeals to the Declaration could be assembled. For example, in his speech on the Dred Scott decision in 1857: "In those [early] days, our Declaration of Independence was held sacred by all and thought to include all; but now, to aid in making the bondage of the Negro universal and eternal, it is assailed and sneered at, and construed, and hawked at and torn, till, if its framers could rise from their graves, they could not at all recognize it."
Or again, in the 1858 debates with Stephen A. Douglas, he said: "I have insisted that, in legislating for new countries, where slavery does not exist, there is no just rule other than that of moral and abstract right! With reference to those new countries, those maxims as to the right of people to 'life, liberty, and the pursuit of happiness' were the just rules to be constantly referred to. There is no misunderstanding this, except by men interested to misunderstand it."

At that place and time, Lincoln spoke in deeply personal tones. (Indeed, he had received warning of a plot to assassinate him when the presidential train passed through Baltimore.) However, what he says should be looked at apart from the fervor with which he says it.

A term from the Greek political lexicon can help us to convey what Lincoln is at some pains to say. In Aristotle's political philosophy, the *politeia* is what gives a particular *polis,* a particular city or state, its identity, its unity, its form. There is no single English word that will serve as a translation of *politeia,* but its meaning can be expressed by speaking of the formative principles or purposes to which a political community is dedicated. Borrowing a term from his philosophical biology, Aristotle speaks analogically of the *politeia* as the "soul" of the body politic, because it is the animating conception that the people have with regard to the meaning and purpose of their political association. The *politeia* is, therefore, antecedent to and deeper than the "constitution." The constitution, which consists in a definition and arrangement of offices, is devised to accord with and be in service to the *politeia.* Substantive legislation under the constitution represents an effort to direct the political life in conformity with the *politeia.* In Aristotle's lexicon, a "revolution" is a change in the *politeia.* Any constitutional change or any major legislative policy in strong and durable violation of the *politeia* would constitute a revolution.

It is clear from the words Lincoln spoke in Independence Hall, and from his persistent invocation of the Declaration in many contexts, that Lincoln held the American *politeia* to have been revealed in the Declaration of Independence. The nation was born—"besouled"—with the Declaration of Independence. Against Stephen Douglas, proposing to allow each new territory to decide for itself whether it wanted the institution of slavery, as well as against Justice Taney, interpreting the Constitution as prohibiting any Federal act preventing the extension of slavery, Lincoln always appealed to the controlling authority of the Declaration, with its pivotal proposition about the equality of men. Any sophistical evasion of that proposition or any policy contravening its exigencies would be a revolutionary breach of the "ancient faith."

That Lincoln began his Address by fixing the birth date of the nation as the year of the Declaration cannot, therefore, be passed over lightly as if it were a mere rhetorical flourish.

> . . . a new nation, conceived in liberty and *dedicated to the proposition that all men are created equal.*

Matthew Arnold, who prided himself on his ability to discern touchstones of great style, is reported to have said that he stopped reading when he came to the phrase about dedication to a "proposition." Lincoln's instinct for style caused him no qualms about the use of that term to designate an object to which men can be dedicated. In traditional logic, a proposition is a sentence setting forth something judged ("held") to be true. In the first line of the second paragraph of the Declaration, that men are equal is held to be true and is declared in a proposition.

Lincoln did not look upon the proposition about human equality as a hypothesis worth examination, or as a postulate for a kind of experiment, or as a beneficent sentiment. For him it was a truth affirmed. He was, of course, obligated to state what he understood the proposition about human equality to mean—what he thought the signers of the Declaration meant.

Shortly after the Dred Scott decision of March 1857, Lincoln learned from a speech by Stephen A. Douglas what Douglas thought the signers had meant. Douglas said:

> No man can vindicate the character, motives, and conduct of the signers of the Declaration of Independence except upon the hypothesis that they referred to the white race alone, and not to the African, when they declared all men to have been created equal; that they were speaking of British subjects on this continent being equal to British subjects born and residing in Great Britain.

In a speech delivered at Springfield, Illinois, June 26, 1857, Lincoln referred to that reading of the proposition by Douglas, found it ludicrous, and could not refrain from somewhat prolonged ridicule of it:

> My good friends, read that carefully over some leisure hour, and ponder well upon it—see what a mere wreck—mangled ruin—it makes of our once glorious Declaration.
>
> "They were speaking of British subjects on this continent being equal to British subjects born and residing in Great Britain!" Why, according to this, not only Negroes but white people outside of Great Britain and America are not spoken of in that instru-

ment. The English, Irish and Scotch, along with white Americans, were included to be sure, but the French, Germans and other white people of the world are all gone to pot along with the Judge's inferior races.

I had thought the Declaration promised something better than the condition of British subjects; but no, it only meant that we should be *equal* to them in their own oppressed and *unequal* condition. According to that, it gave no promise that having kicked off the King and Lords of Great Britain, we should not at once be saddled with a King and Lords of our own.

I had thought the Declaration contemplated the progressive improvement in the condition of all men everywhere; but no, it merely "was adopted for the purpose of justifying the colonists in the eyes of the civilized world in withdrawing their allegiance from the British Crown, and dissolving their connection with the mother country." Why, that object having been effected some eighty years ago, the Declaration is of no practical use now— mere rubbish—old wadding left to rot on the battlefield after the victory is won.

I understand you are preparing to celebrate the "Fourth," tomorrow week. What for? The doings of that day had no reference to the present; and quite half of you are not even descendants of those who were referred to at that day. But I suppose you will celebrate; and will even go so far as to read the Declaration. Suppose after you read it once in the old fashioned way, you read it once more with Judge Douglas' version. It will then run thus: "We hold these truths to be self-evident that all British subjects who were on this continent eighty-one years ago, were created equal to all British subjects born and *then* residing in Great Britain."

And now I appeal to all—to Democrats as well as others,—are you really willing that the Declaration shall be thus frittered away?—thus left no more at most, than an interesting memorial of the dead past? thus shorn of its vitality, and practical value; and left without the *germ* or even the *suggestion* of the individual rights of man in it?

Lincoln was equally outraged by the view expressed by Chief Justice Taney in the Dred Scott decision: "The Constitution recognizes the right of property of the master in a slave, and makes no distinction between that description of property and other property owned by a citizen. [Hence], no tribunal, acting under the authority of the United States, whether it be legislative, executive, or judicial, has a right to draw such a distinction or deny to it the benefit of the provisions and guarantees which have been provided for the protection of private property against the encroachments of the government. . . . The right of property in a slave is distinctly and expressly affirmed in the Constitution."

Against such statements by Douglas and Taney, Lincoln had to offer his own interpretation of the Declaration, and especially to "vindicate the character, motives, and conduct of the signers of the Declaration of Independence" on some other hypothesis than Douglas's, "that they referred to the white race alone." In his speech at Springfield, Illinois, in 1857, Lincoln did precisely that.

Chief Justice Taney, in his opinion in the Dred Scott case, admits that the language of the Declaration is broad enough to include the whole human family, but he and Judge Douglas argue that the authors of that instrument did not intend to include Negroes by the fact that they did not at once actually place them on an equality with the whites. Now this grave argument comes to just nothing at all, by the other fact, that they did not at once, *or ever afterwards,* actually place all white people on an equality with one or another. And this is the staple argument of both the Chief Justice and the Senator for doing this obvious violence to the plain, unmistakable language of the Declaration.

I think the authors of that notable instrument intended to include *all* men, but they did not intend to declare all men equal *in all respects.* They did not mean to say all were equal in color, size, intellect, moral developments, or social capacity. They defined with tolerable distinctness, in what respects they did consider all men created equal—equal with "certain inalienable rights, among which are life, liberty, and the pursuit of happiness." This they said, and this they meant. They did not mean to assert the obvious untruth, that all were then actually enjoying that equality, nor yet, that they were about to confer it immediately upon them. In fact they had no power to confer such a boon. They meant simply to declare the *right,* so that the *enforcement* of it might follow as fast as circumstances should permit.

They meant to set up a standard maxim for free society, which should be familiar to all, and revered by all; constantly looked to, constantly labored for, and even though never perfectly attained, constantly approximated, and thereby constantly spreading and deepening its influence, and augmenting the happiness and value of life to all people of all colors everywhere. The assertion that "all men are created equal" was of no practical use in effecting our separation from Great Britain; and it was placed in the Declaration, not for that, but for future use. Its authors meant it to be, [as,] thank God, it is now proving itself, a stumbling block to those who in after times might seek to turn a free people back into the hateful paths of despotism. They knew the proneness of prosperity to breed tyrants, and they meant when such should re-appear in this fair land and commence their vocation they should find left for them at least one hard nut to crack.

I have now briefly expressed my view of the *meaning* and *objects* of that part of the Declaration of Independence which declares that "all men are created equal."

To return to the Gettysburg Address, it goes on as follows:

> Now we are engaged in a *great* civil war, testing whether that nation or *any nation* so conceived and so dedicated can long endure. We are met on a *great* battlefield of that war.

Was it unseemly to speak of the terrible civil war as a *great* war, of Gettysburg as a *great* battlefield? Lincoln was surely not speaking of the intensity or of the unexpected duration of the war. He was thinking of the magnitude of the issue that was being tested. It was not just whether *this* nation but whether *any* nation so conceived and so dedicated could long endure.

With the words "or any nation," Lincoln raised the question of the worldwide significance of the American model. In his First Inaugural Address, Washington had said: "The sacred fire of liberty and the destiny of the republican model of government are justly considered, perhaps, as *deeply,* as *finally,* staked on the experiment entrusted to the hands of the American people." Washington was echoing what every major revolutionary leader had said about the world meaning of the American Revolution—John Adams, James Madison, Alexander Hamilton, Thomas Jefferson.

Lincoln had many times spoken in the same vein. On the way to his first inauguration, Lincoln addressed the New Jersey Senate. After recalling his boyhood reading, in Parson Weems's *Life of Washington,* of the military struggles around Trenton, he said:

I recollect thinking then, boy even though I was, that there must have been something more than common that those men struggled for. I am exceedingly anxious that that thing which they struggled for—that something even more than National Independence; that something that held out a great promise to all the people of the world for all time to come—I am exceedingly anxious that this Union, the Constitution, and the liberties of the people shall be perpetuated in accordance with the original idea for which that struggle was made, and I shall be most happy indeed if I shall be an humble instrument in the hands of the Almighty, and of this, his almost chosen people, for perpetuating the object of that great struggle.

For Lincoln, what came into being with the war that gave the nation its birth, and held out a great promise to the people of the world for all time to come, was *the* issue in the Civil War. None of the *Federalist Papers* had been more cogent and persuasive than those which argued that progress "towards a more perfect union" was the absolutely necessary condition for a good test of "the experiment entrusted to the hands of the American people." Failing a firm and durable union, the American continent, argued the Federalists, would recapitulate the internecine history of Europe.

Lincoln was convinced that saving the Union was something fateful for all mankind and all future history. Even though, as he said in his Second Inaugural Address, everyone knew that "a peculiar and powerful interest" in the institution of slavery "was *somehow* the cause of the war," the perpetuation of the Union was more important than the fate of slavery in the country.

On that point, Lincoln had been fiercely lucid fourteen months before Gettysburg. An old friend of his, Horace Greeley, in an open letter entitled "The Prayer of Twenty Millions," had accused Lincoln of harboring proslavery sentiments. Lincoln answered him in a personal letter:

As to the policy I "seem to be pursuing," as you say, I have not meant to leave anyone in doubt.

I would save the Union. I would save it the shortest way under the Constitution. The sooner the national authority can be restored; the nearer the Union will be "the Union as it was." If there be those who would not save the Union, unless they could at the same time *save* slavery, I do not agree with them. If there be those who would not save the Union unless they could at the same time *destroy* slavery, I do not agree with them. My paramount object in this struggle *is* to save the Union, and is *not* either to save or to destroy slavery. If I could save the Union without freeing *any* slave I would do it; and if I could save it by freeing *all* the slaves I would do it; and if I could save it by free-ing some and leaving others alone I would also do that. What I do about slavery, and the colored race, I do because I believe it helps to save the Union; and what I forbear, I forbear because I do *not* believe it would help to save the Union. I shall do *less* whenever I shall believe what I am doing hurts the cause, and I shall do *more* whenever I shall believe doing more will help the cause. I shall try to correct errors when shown to be errors; and I shall adopt new views so fast as they shall appear to be true views.

I have here stated my purpose according to my view of *official* duty, and I intend no modification of my oft-expressed personal wish that all men everywhere could be free.

Yours, A. LINCOLN

Despite the reiteration, "saving the Union," taken by itself, did not yield the moral justification for the Civil War. Saving the Union was of such awesome importance only because the preservation of the Union was indispensable to this nation's promotion of "that something," struggled for in the War of Independence, which "held out a great promise to all the people of the world for all time to come." This point becomes firmly clear at the end of the Address.

After words of deep respect for the dead, Lincoln turns to what the living must take from the dead:

> It is rather for us to be here dedicated to the great task remaining before us—that from these honored dead we take increased devotion to that cause for which they gave the last full measure of devotion, that we here highly resolve that these dead shall not have died in vain, *that this nation, under God, shall have a new birth of freedom; and that government of the people, by the people, for the people shall not perish from the earth.*

The "unfinished work," "the great task remaining before us," "that cause for which they gave the last full measure of devotion" —these are articulated in the last two clauses of the Address, which are statements of purpose. The first purpose concerns *"this"* nation —that *it* "shall have a new birth of freedom." The second concerns the historical future of an idea—the idea of democracy—that it "shall not perish from the earth."

Some, if not all, of the revolutionary leaders believed that somehow, by the very circumstances of the nation's birth, the idea of democracy was held in trust by America. For Lincoln it was precisely that trust which was being tested in a great Civil War.

Lincoln formulated the idea of democracy in what has become a world-famous trinity of prepositional phrases:

> . . . **government of the people, by the people, for the people** . . .

This tripartite formula has acquired widespread talismanic power. It has always been invoked by the American people as an inspired formula. However, if we take this triad of prepositional phrases as a compressed formulation of the idea of democracy, it is necessary to ask a number of questions which aim at explicating its meaning.

We are led to such questions by the comments of Bertrand De Jouvenel, a distinguished French political philosopher and political scientist. In a paper entitled *What is Democracy?*, written in 1958 for a conference on "Representative Government and Public Liberties in the New States," De Jouvenel found Lincoln's "formula" a ludicrous failure, even something of a hoax.[2] De Jouvenel's findings are useful as yielding the questions that we must ask about Lincoln's formula.

In regard to *"government of the people,"* De Jouvenel writes: "Let me first note that any *de facto* authority, habitually obeyed and acknowledged by a people, is its government; the first term, therefore, merely tells us that a government must be obeyed and acknowledged by the people; if not, it is not the government of the people, but then it is no government at all."

In regard to *"government by the people,"* De Jouvenel interprets it to mean that "all decisions are jointly taken by all members of

[2] Another denigration of Lincoln's "formula" can be found in Giovanni Sartori's *Democratic Theory* (pp. 26–27, Praeger, 1965). Sartori writes: "It is symptomatic that [Lincoln's] aphorism defies analysis and poses insoluble problems of interpretation. . . . The truth is that Lincoln's words have stylistic impetus rather than logical meaning. As they stand they constitute, strictly speaking, an inexplicable proposition."

the community assembled for that purpose"; this, he says, describes
"no government as we know it"; it is applicable only to ancient
Athens and a few anomalous, small, short-lived communities in
Western history.

In regard to *"government for the people,"* De Jouvenel writes:
"The last term reminds us that a government has a moral obligation of seeking the good of the people; this is valid for a government of whatever origin or form." Accordingly, in his view,
Lincoln's third term in no way catches something distinctive
about democracy.

Our response to De Jouvenel must begin by conceding that the
only way to counter his attack is by treating Lincoln's triad of
phrases as an *oracle*—compressed, cryptic, expressing deep truths.

. . . government *of* the people . . .

Grammarians have long since noted an ambiguity in the use of
the genitive case. On the one hand, the phrase, "the love of God"
(by man) can be used to designate the love that is directed to God
as an object of love. The genitive is then an *objective genitive*. On
the other hand, "the love of God" can be used to designate the love
that God has for man. The genitive is then a *possessive genitive*.

Lincoln's oracular "of" is what might be called a "deliberate
double-genitive." He did not need to be told by De Jouvenel that
"government" is a relative term, so that where there is "government," there has to be a "governed." Democracy is not anarchy. It
involves government and therefore those who are governed—the
subjects or objects of government. (Even in so-called "direct democracy," there is a distinction between the people-as-governing and
the people-as-governed.) Hence the phrase "government of the
people" involves an objective genitive: The people are governed.

However, in a democracy that is genuine, the people are governed by a government that is *theirs,* by a government that belongs
to them, as an instrument belongs to its user. It is, therefore, necessary to distinguish between a people conceived as submitting to a
government that claims to derive its authority and power from
sources which are wholly extraneous to them (as is the case in an
absolute monarchy or despotism), and a people conceived as under
a government that derives its authority and power from their consent.

Given the privileges of the oracular style, Lincoln's first prepositional phrase contains a possessive genitive at the same time that it contains an objective genitive.[3] That possessive genitive calls attention to the fundamental distinction between constitutional and despotic government—a government of laws as contrasted with a government by men. Constitutional government is government that derives its authority and power from the consent of the people, and is therefore *their* government. Constitutional government takes different forms: It is oligarchical or democratic depending on the meaning of the words "the people" in the phrase "government of the people," as well as in the other two phrases associated with it. If "the people" stands for the whole human population of the political community—all except the few who can be justly excepted, such as infants or hospitalized mental incompetents—then we have the specific form of government known as constitutional democracy. Lincoln's adherence to the proposition about human equality in the Declaration, together with its consequential avowal of the possession by all of the same inherent and unalienable human rights, must persuade us that when he spoke of "government of the people, by the people, and for the people," he had constitutional democracy in mind, not merely as one specific form of government among others, but as the only just form of government—more just than a constitutional oligarchy in which the consenting people are a privileged few, and much more just than a despotic or absolute government in which the people are the subjects of a government that is in no sense theirs because it in no way involves their consent or participation.

The significance of the possessive genitive in the initial phrase— "government of the people"—can be summarized in the following propositions that any defender of the rightness of constitutional government should affirm as true. They provide us with the defini-

---

[3] In two passages, often considered as probable sources in his memory for Lincoln's triad of phrases, the *possessive genitive* had made a firm appearance. Daniel Webster, in his famous Reply to Hayne, a speech Lincoln is known to have read and valued, used these words: "The people's government, made for the people, made by the people, and answerable to the people." In a major opinion, *M'Culloch* v. *Maryland,* Chief Justice John Marshall had written: "The government of the Union is emphatically and truly a government of the people. In form and in substance it emanates from them. Its powers are granted by them, and are to be exercised directly on them and for their benefit."

tive solution of a problem that has persisted throughout the whole tradition of Western political thought—the problem about the source of the authority and the grounds for the legitimacy of governments.

1. Authority is not possessed by a government merely as a result of the *de facto* submission of the governed to the power it is able to exert over them.

2. A government has genuine authority—the right to govern— only when such authority is conferred on it, or transmitted to it, by acts of the people as its consenting constituents, originating, constitutive acts, interim acts of consent, and periodically recurring electoral acts.

3. While such authority is possessed and exercised by the office-holders or officials in a constitutional government, it is held and exercised by them in dependence on the people to whom it principally and inalienably belongs.

4. Just as in the physical world, an instrumental cause, such as the painter's brush, has its causal power imparted to it by the principal cause, the painter's art, so in the political realm, the governing bodies in a constitutional government function as an instrument empowered by the people.

. . . government . . . *by* the people . . .

At the time that Lincoln spoke, he was the head of a government in a not-all-that-small society. It is way off the mark for De Jouvenel or anybody else to suggest that Lincoln, in a spasm of rhetorical excitement, was trying to suggest that the government of the United States was a government-of-everybody-by-everybody—government by the assembly of all the citizens, as in Athens or in a New England town.

The leaders of the revolutionary and constitutional period had spoken of "self-government," even though, because of the size of the society, such government would involve representation in a legislative body rather than the direct participation of the citizens in a public assembly. In *Federalist* #39, Madison wrote: "It is evident that no other form of government would be reconcilable with the genius of the people of America; with the fundamental principles of the Revolution; or with that honorable determination which animates every votary of freedom, to rest all our political experiments on the capacity of mankind for self-government." The fathers of the republic were not intimidated by the paradoxes often supposed to lie in the term "self-government." Those paradoxes, largely verbal, can be discounted by considering the relation between rulers and ruled under a constitutional government.

Aristotle had pointed out, many centuries before, that under constitutional government the citizens rule and are ruled in turn. They are both rulers and ruled. The office of citizenship is the primary and permanent office in a constitutional regime; all other offices, including that of the chief magistrate, are secondary offices, to which citizens are eligible and which some of them fill for a period of time, to resume their status as private citizens when they leave public office.

The people—the body of the citizens constituting the ruling class —must, therefore, be regarded as the permanent principal rulers in a constitutional democracy. The officeholders, the public officials or magistrates to whom the administration of the government is entrusted while they hold office, are by contrast with the citizens the transient instrumental rulers, directly or indirectly elected by the people and responsible to them. This relationship between private citizens and public officials may be concealed by the verbal habit of referring to officialdom—the collection of temporary officeholders or magistrates—as "the government." We speak of a change of government when one set of officials leaves office to be replaced by another; but actually it is only a change in the administration of the government. The framework of government remains unchanged, and in that framework the citizens remain the principal rulers and the temporary occupants of public offices function as their instruments of self-government.[4]

Under the Constitution of the United States, officeholders wield whatever authority and power are vested in their office by the Constitution. Neither the authority nor the power belongs to them personally, but rather to the office they hold. They exercise it only as officeholders. Their exercise of it is subject, even concurrently

[4] Lincoln's language in his First Inaugural is worth noticing: "Doing this [taking care that the laws of the Union be faithfully executed in all the states] I deem to be only a simple duty on my part; and I shall perform it, so far as practicable, unless *my rightful masters, the American people,* shall withhold the requisite means or in some authoritative manner direct the contrary."

with that exercise, to such critical inspection and control by the people as will not render them impotent for the performance of their designated instrumental functions. In addition, they are liable to impeachment and removal from office when they exceed the constitutional authority vested in their office or usurp powers not allotted to them, as well as when they commit other high crimes and misdemeanors. A constitutional government is thus a government of laws in the sense that no man is above the law and no man has political authority or legitimate power except that which is conferred upon him by the people who govern themselves through the services of their political instruments—public officials or office-holders.

To say that constitutional democracy is both government *of* the people and government *by* the people is to say that the people are both the constituents of government through acts of consent to the constitution which they have adopted as the framework of government, and also that they are enfranchised citizens participating through the exercise of their suffrage in self-government—not directly, but indirectly through their representatives upon whom they have conferred the authority to administer the functions of government. In the last analysis, government in a democracy, even if it is through representatives rather than through the direct action of the citizens, is government by the people.

. . . government . . . *for* the people . . .

As De Jouvenel pointed out, the phrase, taken by itself, refers to something that is common to all forms of government which are good or just; namely, that they consist in government for the public good, the good of the governed or the community as a whole, not government in the service of the private interests of those who administer the functions of government.

However, democratic governments are charged with doing more *for* the people than are benevolent monarchies and wise aristocracies, precisely because constitutional democracy is fundamentally an experiment in self-government. Just as government *by* the people takes on a special significance from the fact that it is, first of all, the people's government, so too government *for* the people draws its full force from the antecedent fact that it is both government *of* and also *by* the people.

The idea of democracy presupposes that all men are not only equal under the law but equal as well in their claim to the rights of life, liberty, and the pursuit of happiness that a just government must try to make secure for them. Accordingly, democratic governments have an obligation that is inherent in the idea of democracy but alien to the idea of monarchy and the idea of aristocracy—the obligation to secure for all the rights to which all have an equal claim.

The Preamble's statement of the purposes of our government enunciates an articulation of the common good. Of the six purposes or objectives of government there stated, the last calls for something that is specific to a constitutional democracy and that enlarges —and immeasurably deepens—the conception of the common good. No other form of government is called upon by its constituents "to secure the blessings of liberty for ourselves and our posterity."

Being a limited government, a constitutional democracy is restrained from invading certain precincts of purely personal liberty. Being accountable to the people, it must not only respect, but it must also strive to enhance, those freedoms which the people need for the mature, critical control of government—freedom of thought, freedom of expression, freedom of association and of public assembly, freedom to dissent and to petition for the redress of grievances.

Because the idea of democracy entails such additional things that a democratic government is obliged to do *for* the people, democracy is pre-eminently "government *for* the people," and, therefore, once again in Jefferson's words, "the only truly just form of government."

If the idea of democracy became at this nation's birth something it regarded itself as holding in trust for the world and for the future, and if Lincoln's oracular triad of prepositional phrases indeed epitomizes that idea, then we have not been wrong in regarding Lincoln's last ten words as the focal point of the American Testament.

APPENDIX

Universal Declaration of Human Rights

———

Preamble

Whereas recognition of the inherent dignity and of the equal and inalienable rights of all members of the human family is the foundation of freedom, justice and peace in the world,

Whereas disregard and contempt for human rights have resulted in barbarous acts which have outraged the conscience of mankind, and the advent of a world in which human beings shall enjoy freedom of speech and belief and freedom from fear and want has been proclaimed as the highest aspiration of the common people,

Whereas it is essential, if man is not to be compelled to have recourse, as a last resort, to rebellion against tyranny and oppression, that human rights should be protected by the rule of law,

Whereas it is essential to promote the development of friendly relations between nations,

Whereas the peoples of the United Nations have in the Charter reaffirmed their faith in fundamental human rights, in the dignity and worth of the human person and in the equal rights of men and women and have determined to promote social progress and better standards of life in larger freedom,

Whereas Member States have pledged themselves to achieve, in co-

SOURCE: Part A of Res. 217 (III), approved by the General Assembly on Dec. 10, 1948. Text as given in U.N. General Assembly, Third Session, First Part, *Official Records,* "Resolutions," pp. 71–77.

operation with the United Nations, the promotion of universal respect for and observance of human rights and fundamental freedoms,

Whereas a common understanding of these rights and freedoms is of the greatest importance for the full realization of this pledge,

Now, therefore,

The General Assembly

Proclaims this Universal Declaration of Human Rights as a common standard of achievement for all peoples and all nations, to the end that every individual and every organ of society, keeping this Declaration constantly in mind, shall strive by teaching and education to promote respect for these rights and freedoms and by progressive measures, national and international, to secure their universal and effective recognition and observance, both among the peoples of Member States themselves and among the peoples of territories under their jurisdiction.

Article 1

All human beings are born free and equal in dignity and rights. They are endowed with reason and conscience and should act towards one another in a spirit of brotherhood.

Article 2

Everyone is entitled to all the rights and freedoms set forth in this Declaration, without distinction of any kind, such as race, colour, sex, language, religion, political or other opinion, national or social origin, property, birth or other status.

Furthermore, no distinction shall be made on the basis of the political, jurisdictional or international status of the country or territory to which a person belongs, whether it be independent, trust, non-self-governing or under any other limitation of sovereignty.

Article 3

Everyone has the right to life, liberty and the security of person.

Article 4

No one shall be held in slavery or servitude; slavery and the slave trade shall be prohibited in all their forms.

Article 5

No one shall be subjected to torture or to cruel, inhuman or degrading treatment or punishment.

Article 6

Everyone has the right to recognition everywhere as a person before the law.

Article 7

All are equal before the law and are entitled without any discrimination to equal protection of the law. All are entitled to equal protection against any discrimination in violation of this Declaration and against any incitement to such discrimination.

Article 8

Everyone has the right to an effective remedy by the competent national tribunals for acts violating the fundamental rights granted him by the constitution or by law.

Article 9

No one shall be subjected to arbitrary arrest, detention or exile.

Article 10

Everyone is entitled in full equality to a fair and public hearing by an independent and impartial tribunal, in the determination of his rights and obligations and of any criminal charge against him.

Article 11

1. Everyone charged with a penal offense has the right to be presumed innocent until proved guilty according to law in a public trial at which he has had all the guarantees necessary for his defence.

2. No one shall be held guilty of any penal offence on account of any act or omission which did not constitute a penal offence, under national or international law, at the time when it was committed. Nor shall a heavier penalty be imposed than the one that was applicable at the time the penal offence was committed.

Article 12

No one shall be subjected to arbitrary interference with his privacy, family, home or correspondence, nor to attacks upon his honour and reputation. Everyone has the right to the protection of the law against such interference or attacks.

Article 13

1. Everyone has the right to freedom of movement and residence within the borders of each State.

2. Everyone has the right to leave any country, including his own, and to return to his country.

Article 14

1. Everyone has the right to seek and to enjoy in other countries asylum from persecution.

2. This right may not be invoked in the case of prosecutions genuinely arising from nonpolitical crimes or from acts contrary to the purposes and principles of the United Nations.

Article 15

1. Everyone has the right to a nationality.

2. No one shall be arbitrarily deprived of his nationality nor denied the right to change his nationality.

Article 16

1. Men and women of full age, without any limitation due to race, nationality or religion, have the right to marry and to found a family. They are entitled to equal rights as to marriage, during marriage and at its dissolution.

2. Marriage shall be entered into only with the free and full consent of the intending spouses.

3. The family is the natural and fundamental group unit of society and is entitled to protection by society and the State.

Article 17

1. Everyone has the right to own property alone as well as in association with others.

2. No one shall be arbitrarily deprived of his property.

Article 18

Everyone had the right to freedom of thought, conscience and religion; this right includes freedom to change his religion or belief, and freedom, either alone or in community with others and in public or private, to manifest his religion or belief in teaching, practice, worship and observance.

Article 19

Everyone has the right to freedom of opinion and expression; this right includes freedom to hold opinions without interference and to seek, receive and impart information and ideas through any media and regardless of frontiers.

Article 20

1. Everyone has the right to freedom of peaceful assembly and association.

2. No one may be compelled to belong to an association.

Article 21

1. Everyone has the right to take part in the government of his country, directly or through freely chosen representatives.

2. Everyone has the right of equal access to public service in his country.

3. The will of the people shall be the basis of the authority of government; this will shall be expressed in periodic and genuine elections

which shall be by universal and equal suffrage and shall be held by secret vote or by equivalent free voting procedures.

Article 22

Everyone, as a member of society, has the right to social security and is entitled to realization, through national effort and international cooperation and in accordance with the organization and resources of each state, of the economic, social and cultural rights indispensable for his dignity and the free development of his personality.

Article 23

1. Everyone has the right to work, to free choice of employment, to just and favourable conditions of work and to protection against unemployment.

2. Everyone, without any discrimination, has the right to equal pay for equal work.

3. Everyone who works has the right to just and favourable remuneration ensuring for himself and his family an existence worthy of human dignity, and supplemented, if necessary, by other means of social protection.

4. Everyone has the right to form and to join trade unions for the protection of his interests.

Article 24

Everyone has the right to rest and leisure, including reasonable limitation of working hours and periodic holidays with pay.

Article 25

1. Everyone has the right to a standard of living adequate for the health and well-being of himself and of his family, including food, clothing, housing and medical care and necessary social services, and the right to security in the event of unemployment, sickness, disability, widowhood, old age or other lack of livelihood in circumstances beyond his control.

2. Motherhood and childhood are entitled to special care and assistance. All children, whether born in or out of wedlock, shall enjoy the same social protection.

Article 26

1. Everyone has the right to education. Education shall be free, at least in the elementary and fundamental stages. Elementary education shall be compulsory. Technical and professional education shall be made generally available and higher education shall be equally accessible to all on the basis of merit.

2. Education shall be directed to the full development of the human personality and to the strengthening of respect for human rights and fundamental freedoms. It shall promote understanding, tolerance and friendship among all nations, racial or religious groups, and shall further the activities of the United Nations for the maintenance of peace.

3. Parents have a prior right to choose the kind of education that shall be given to their children.

Article 27

1. Everyone has the right freely to participate in the cultural life of the community, to enjoy the arts and to share in scientific advancement and its benefits.

2. Everyone has the right to the protection of the moral and material interests resulting from any scientific, literary or artistic production of which he is the author.

Article 28

Everyone is entitled to a social and international order in which the rights and freedoms set forth in this Declaration can be fully realized.

Article 29

1. Everyone has duties to the community in which alone the free and full development of his personality is possible.

2. In the exercise of his rights and freedoms, everyone shall be subject only to such limitations as are determined by law solely for the purpose of securing due recognition and respect for the rights and freedoms of others and of meeting the just requirements of morality, public order and the general welfare in a democratic society.

3. These rights and freedoms may in no case be exercised contrary to the purposes and principles of the United Nations.

Article 30

Nothing in this Declaration may be interpreted as implying for any State, group or person any right to engage in any activity or to perform any act aimed at the destruction of any of the rights and freedoms set forth herein.

Glossary

ADAMS, JOHN (1735–1826), second President of the U.S. Born in Braintree (now Quincy), Massachusetts, October 19, 1735. Graduated from Harvard 1755. Admitted to the bar 1758. Drafted protest against the Stamp Act for Braintree 1765. Became a member of the colonial legislature in 1771 and of the Continental Congress in 1774. Served on the committee charged with drafting the Declaration of Independence. Mission to France 1778. Member of the Massachusetts Constitutional Convention 1779. Participated in negotiations that ended the revolutionary war. Minister to the Netherlands 1780–85 and to Great Britain 1785–88. Vice-President of the U.S. 1789–97, and President 1797–1801. Appointed John Marshall Chief Justice of U.S. Supreme Court as one of his last acts in office. Passed his retirement in Braintree until his death on July 4, 1826.

ADAMS, JOHN QUINCY (1767–1848), sixth President of the U.S. Born in Braintree (now Quincy), Massachusetts, July 11, 1767. Traveled frequently with his father, John Adams, in latter's conduct of foreign affairs. Graduated from Harvard 1787. Admitted to the bar 1790. U.S. Minister to the Netherlands 1794–96 and to Berlin 1796–1801. Elected to the Massachusetts legislature in 1802 and to the U.S. Senate in 1803. Minister to Russia 1809–14 and chairman of U.S. peace commission at Ghent in 1814 to negotiate the end of the War of 1812. Minister to Great Britain 1814–17, when he became Secretary of State under President Monroe. Elected President in contested election of 1824, but defeated by Andrew Jackson for a second term in 1828. Elected to the House of Representatives in 1830 and served there until his death on February 23, 1848.

ARTICLES OF CONFEDERATION. On motion by Richard Henry Lee, second Continental Congress on June 7, 1776, appointed a committee to draw up a plan of union. Draft, written by John Dickinson of Pennsylvania, presented to the Congress June 12. Adopted in much revised form 1777. Ratified by all the states effective 1781. As an instrument of government it gave Congress authority without enforcement powers, leading to general breakdown of governmental operations by 1786.

BARLOW, JOEL (1754–1812), author, poet, and diplomat. Born in Redding, Connecticut, March 24, 1754. Graduated from Yale 1778. Chaplain in the Revolutionary army 1780–83. Admitted to the bar 1786. Wrote poetry for the *Anarchiad* 1786–87 and published his nine-volume work, *The Vision of Columbus,* in 1787. In 1788 he went to Europe, where he remained for several years, becoming a citizen of France in 1792, during French Revolution. Wrote a number of political tracts, notably 1792 *Advice to the Privileged Orders,* as well as 1796 poetical work *The Hasty Pudding.* U.S. Consul in Algiers 1795–97. Returned to U.S. in 1805. Appointed Minister to France, he was with Napoleon and his troops in Russia during retreat from Moscow. Died in Poland on December 24, 1812.

BERNARD, SIR FRANCIS (1712–79), colonial official. Born in England, July 1712. Educated at Oxford. Studied law at Middle Temple in London. Admitted to the bar 1737. Governor of colony of New Jersey 1758–60. Appointed Governor of Massachusetts 1760. His administration was a turbulent one, disturbed by the troubles between the colony and England. Disliked the Stamp Act but enforced it. His plan for reorganization of New England further alienated colonists. Increasing unpopularity led to recall; returned to England August 1769. Retired to Aylesbury, where he died on June 16, 1779.

BILL OF RIGHTS. Set of amendments to new U.S. Constitution drawn up by first Congress in response to criticism of Constitution because it lacked guarantees of citizens' rights. Twelve amendments, generally modeled after Virginia Declaration of Rights (1776), were presented to the states for adoption on September 25, 1789. Ten of the twelve, making up the present Bill of Rights, were ratified by December 15, 1791.

BOUCHER, JONATHAN (1738–1804), clergyman. Born in Cumberland, England, in 1738. Ordained an Anglican priest. Lived in Virginia 1759–

75. A vehement opponent of American independence, he returned to England 1775. Published his opinions on the American Revolution under the title *A View of the Causes and Consequences of the American Revolution* (1797). Died in Epsom, England, on April 27, 1804.

BURKE, EDMUND (1729–97), public official. Born in Dublin, January 12, 1729. Graduated from Trinity College, Dublin, 1748. Studied law at Middle Temple in London. Wrote, traveled, and worked at various jobs 1748–65. Among early published works were *Vindication of Natural Society* (1756) and *Account of the European Settlements in America* (1757). Editor of *Annual Register* for thirty years beginning 1759. Elected to Parliament 1765. Called for repeal of the Stamp Act. Re-elected to Parliament from Bristol 1774. Continued to support the American colonies by speech and tract, most notably in *Speech on Conciliation with America* (1775) and *Letter to the Sheriffs of Bristol on the Affairs of America* (1777). Following the outbreak of the French Revolution he published an aristocratic manifesto entitled *Reflections on the Revolution in France*. Retired from Parliament 1794. Died in Beaconsfield, England, on July 9, 1797.

BUTLER, PIERCE (1744–1822), public official. Born in County Carlow, Ireland, July 11, 1744. Settled in South Carolina 1771. Served in the state legislature 1778–82, 1784–89. Elected to the Continental Congress 1787. Delegate to the Constitutional Convention of 1787. Proponent of a strong federal government. Elected to U.S. Senate 1789, and re-elected 1792; resigned 1796. Returned to the Senate to fill out unexpired term 1802–6. Died in Philadelphia on February 15, 1822.

COMMITTEES OF CORRESPONDENCE. Local colonial groups under the authority of the legislatures, with the task of dealing with a colony's agents in London. Post-1770 revolutionary ferment led to a greatly increased number of such groups, usually local and unofficial, that provided an inter-colonial core of leadership for opposition to British policies. Massachusetts alone had at least eighty such committees, the earliest of which was formed under the leadership of Samuel Adams in November 1772. Virginia's committee was appointed by the legislature the following March. These committees exchanged information and correlated anti-British policies. As a major agent of colonial unity, the committees promoted the calling of the first Continental Congress in 1774.

CONSTITUTION, RATIFICATION OF U.S. The instrument of government drafted by the Constitutional Convention, May 25–September 17, 1787, was transmitted to Congress September 17 and to the states for ratification September 28. Delaware was first (December 7, 1787) and New Hampshire ninth (June 21, 1788) to ratify. Two largest states, Virginia and New York, followed suit in June and July 1788, respectively. New government went into effect March 4, 1789. North Carolina ratified November 21, 1789, and Rhode Island May 29, 1790.

CONSTITUTIONAL CONVENTION OF 1787. Weakness of the Articles of Confederation and interstate rivalries led to calling of Annapolis Convention, September 11, 1786. Five states there represented decided on federal convention to revise the Articles. Constitutional Convention met in Philadelphia, May 25–September 17, 1788. Of seventy-four elected delegates, fifty-five attended at one time or another. Rhode Island not represented. Members, meeting in secret, decided on creating a new instrument of government. Finished product signed by a majority of attending members on September 17 and presented to states for ratification (see Constitution, ratification of U.S.).

CONTINENTAL CONGRESS (1774–89). Collective name for bodies of colonial, then state, delegates meeting to conduct the affairs of the rebelling colonies and the independent nation. Operated without an instrument of government until ratification of Articles of Confederation 1781. First Continental Congress (1774–75) convened September 5, 1774, at Philadelphia, with fifty-six members, each state with one vote. Second Continental Congress (1775–76) convened May 10, 1775. Issued Declaration of Independence July 4, 1776, and drafted Articles of Confederation.

DAVIS, DAVID (1815–86), Associate Justice of the U.S. Supreme Court. Born in Cecil County, Maryland, March 9, 1815. Graduated from Kenyon College 1832 and from Yale Law School 1835. Settled in Bloomington, Illinois, 1836. Elected to state legislature 1844. Member of state constitutional convention 1847. Elected judge of Eighth Illinois Circuit Court 1848. A strong supporter of Lincoln at 1860 Republican convention. Appointed to U.S. Supreme Court 1862. Best-known decision while on the bench was his majority opinion in *Ex parte Milligan*, denying military the right to try civilians in nonmilitary areas even in wartime. Nominated for presidency in 1872 on Labor Reform ticket.

Resigned from Court in 1877, after being elected to U.S. Senate from Illinois. Remained in Senate until 1883. Died in Bloomington, Illinois, on June 26, 1886.

DECLARATION OF INDEPENDENCE. The Resolution of Independence was introduced to the second Continental Congress by Richard Henry Lee on June 7, 1776. Congress appointed committee of Thomas Jefferson (author of document), John Adams, Benjamin Franklin, Roger Sherman, and Robert Livingston to write Declaration justifying Resolution. Declaration submitted to Congress for debate June 28. Adopted July 4 and signed by John Hancock; eventually signed by fifty-five other patriots.

DOUGLAS, STEPHEN ARNOLD (1813–61), public official. Born in Brandon, Vermont, April 23, 1813. Moved to Illinois 1833. Admitted to the bar 1834. Elected to state legislature 1836. Illinois secretary of state 1840–41. Judge of state supreme court 1841–43. Served in U.S. House of Representatives 1843–47. Elected to U.S. Senate 1847 and served there until his death. Played major role in Compromise of 1850 and was largely responsible for Kansas-Nebraska Act of 1854, repealing Missouri Compromise. During re-election campaign of 1858 he engaged in a series of debates throughout Illinois with his opponent, Abraham Lincoln. Re-elected to Senate, he ran for presidency in 1860 with the support of Northern Democrats. Died in Chicago on June 3, 1861.

DRED SCOTT v. SANDFORD, decision of U.S. Supreme Court written by Chief Justice Roger B. Taney and handed down March 6, 1857. Declared (1) the Missouri Compromise unconstitutional, (2) Negroes not citizens and thus unable to sue in federal courts, (3) residence of a slave in a free state did not grant freedom. Also denied Congress the right to legislate on slavery in the territories. Decision thus negated Stephen A. Douglas's theory of "popular sovereignty" as embodied in Kansas-Nebraska Act of 1854.

DUCHÉ, JACOB (1737–98), clergyman. Born in Philadelphia, January 31, 1737. Graduated from College of Philadelphia 1757. One year of study at Cambridge University in England. Entered parish ministry of Anglican church; ordained in England 1762. Served the united parishes of St. Peter's and Christ Church in Philadelphia. Patriotic fervor earned him appointment as chaplain of the first Continental Congress. Once independence was declared, he turned Loyalist. Deemed a traitor, he went to England to live 1777. Returned to the U.S. 1792. Died in Philadelphia on January 3, 1798.

DULANY, DANIEL (1722–97), lawyer. Born in Annapolis, Maryland, June 28, 1722. Educated in England. Admitted to the bar 1747. Member of the Maryland legislature 1751–54, 1756. Served on colony's ruling council 1757–75. Denied legality of Stamp Act in tract, *Considerations on the Propriety of Imposing Taxes in the British Colonies* 1765. Remained a Loyalist during the revolutionary war. Died in Baltimore on March 17, 1797.

ENGLISH BILL OF RIGHTS. Promulgated 1689 as "Act declaring the rights and liberties of the subject and settling the succession of the Crown." An outcome of the "Glorious Revolution" of 1688. Incorporated provisions of the Declaration of Rights (1688) to which William and Mary had agreed upon accession to the English throne.

FEDERALIST PAPERS. Series of eighty-five articles co-authored by Alexander Hamilton, James Madison, and John Jay in 1787–88 to persuade New York ratifying convention to approve new Constitution. Seventy-eight of the articles published in newspapers at the time under pseudonym "Publius." Collected in book form 1788.

FRANKLIN, BENJAMIN (1706–90), publisher, author, inventor, diplomat, and public official. Born in Boston, January 17, 1706. Served as apprentice printer for his brother James 1821–23. Moved to Philadelphia in 1723, where he worked as a printer. Became owner of Pennsylvania *Gazette* 1730; published *Poor Richard's Almanack* 1732–58. Established Library Company of Philadelphia 1731. One of the founders of American Philosophical Society 1743. Clerk of Pennsylvania Assembly 1736–51, and a delegate to the Assembly 1751–64. Published *Experiments and Observations on Electricity* 1751. Deputy postmaster general for the colonies 1753–74. Represented Pennsylvania at Albany Conference in 1754, where he drafted plan for intercolonial union. Represented colony in England 1757–62 and while there published influential tract *The Interest of Great Britain Considered with Regard to Her Colonies* (1760). Following Stamp Act (1765) attempted to conciliate differences with England until Parliament passed

"Coercive Acts" of 1774. Became delegate to second Continental Congress 1775 and was member of committee that drafted Declaration of Independence. American representative in Paris during revolutionary war and a negotiator for treaty of peace. Returned to America 1785 and elected president of Pennsylvania executive council. Delegate to Constitutional Convention of 1787. Lived in retirement until his death in Philadelphia on April 17, 1790.

GEORGE III (1738–1820), King of Great Britain 1760–1820. Born in London, June 4, 1738. Reign began during Seven Years' War and saw loss of American colonies, the French Revolution, the Napoleonic Wars, and the War of 1812. Determined to maintain royal prerogatives, yet was unable to rule at times owing to episodes of insanity or some other disorder. Prince of Wales named regent 1811. The King went into seclusion until his death at Windsor Castle on January 29, 1820.

GERRY, ELBRIDGE (1744–1814), Vice-President of the U.S. Born in Marblehead, Massachusetts, July 17, 1744. Graduated from Harvard 1762. Member of Massachusetts General Court 1772–74 and of provincial congress 1774–75. Elected to Continental Congress 1776 and served until 1785, except for two-year absence 1781–82. Signed the Declaration of Independence 1776. Elected to Massachusetts House of Representatives 1786 and was a delegate to Constitutional Convention of 1787. Served in U.S. House of Representatives 1789–93. Served with John Marshall and Charles C. Pinckney as commissioner to France 1797. Ran for Governor of Massachusetts several times before finally being elected 1810 and re-elected 1811. Elected Vice-President under James Madison 1812. Served until his death in Washington, D.C., on November 23, 1814.

GETTYSBURG ADDRESS. Short speech given by President Lincoln as part of dedication ceremonies at military cemetery at Gettysburg, Pennsylvania, November 19, 1863.

GREELEY, HORACE (1811–72), editor and reformer. Born near Amherst, New Hampshire, February 3, 1811. Settled in New York City in 1831 as a printer. Founded *New York Tribune* in 1841. Espoused numerous reform movements, especially antislavery. Joined Republican Party in 1854 and supported Lincoln in 1860, but only in a halfhearted way. Disagreed with Lincoln's war policies and engaged in secret negotiations of his own to end the Civil War. His lenient Reconstruction ideas made him unpopular. Ran for presidency against Grant in 1872 on coalition of Liberal Republican and Democratic tickets. After losing election decisively, he died in Pleasantville, New York, on November 29, 1872.

HAMILTON, ALEXANDER (1755–1804), public official. Born on the island of Nevis in the Caribbean, January 11, 1755. Attended King's (now Columbia) College, New York City, 1772. Active in pro-independence cause from 1774 on. Joined Continental Army. Served as Washington's aide-de-camp 1777–81. Settled in New York 1783. A proponent of a strong federal government, he attended Annapolis Convention of 1786. Delegate to Constitutional Convention of 1787. Along with James Madison and John Jay, wrote *Federalist Papers* in 1788 supporting new Constitution. Secretary of the Treasury under Washington 1789–95. Practiced law in New York after 1795. Inspector general of the army 1799. Supported Jefferson in election of 1800. His opposition to Aaron Burr's campaign for governor of New York in 1804 led to duel between the two men on January 11, 1804, at Weehawken, New Jersey. Hamilton was wounded and died the following day.

HENRY, PATRICK (1736–99), public official. Born in Hanover County, Virginia, May 29, 1736. Admitted to the bar 1760 and attained prominence as a lawyer. Elected to Virginia House of Burgesses 1765. Passing of Stamp Act by Parliament (1765) made him vocal opponent of British policy. Member of Virginia's first committee of correspondence and a ·delegate to first and second Continental Congresses. Governor of Virginia 1776–79, 1784–86. Member of state legislature 1780–84, 1787–90. Opposed both Constitutional Convention of 1787 and ratification of new Constitution. Strongly supported the Bill of Rights that was added to the Constitution during Washington's first term. Retired to law practice in 1788. Elected to state legislature again in 1799, but died on June 6, in Charlotte County, before taking office.

HUTCHINSON, THOMAS (1711–80), public official. Born in Boston, September 9, 1711. Graduated from Harvard 1727. As wealthy merchant he was elected to Boston's Board of Selectmen 1737 and to Massachusetts General Court the same year. Served on the court until 1749. Member of Massachusetts Council until 1766. Delegate to Albany Convention 1754. Appointed Lieutenant Governor 1758 and Massachusetts Chief Justice 1760. Upheld right of Parliament to legislate for colonies. Became acting Governor 1769 and was appointed to the position 1771. His enforcement of British rights led to Boston Tea Party of 1773. Left for England 1774 to advise British Government on colonial affairs. Died in Bromptom, England, on June 3, 1780.

JAY, JOHN (1745–1829), Chief Justice of the U.S. Supreme Court. Born in New York City, December 12, 1745. Graduated from King's (now Columbia) College 1764. Admitted to the bar 1768. Elected to first Continental Congress 1774. Opposed Declaration of Independence but supported revolutionary war. Member of New York provincial congress 1776–77. Chief Justice of New York 1777–79. Minister plenipotentiary to Spain 1779–82. Member of U.S. peace commission 1782–83 in Paris. Secretary of Foreign Affairs 1783–89. A supporter of the new Constitution, he was one of the authors of the *Federalist Papers* in 1788. First Chief Justice of U.S. Supreme Court 1789–95. Minister to Great Britain 1794 to negotiate treaty that bears his name. Elected Governor of New York 1795. Retired in 1801 to Bedford, New York, where he died on May 17, 1829.

JEFFERSON, THOMAS (1743–1826), third President of the U.S. Born in Albemarle County, Virginia, April 13, 1743. Graduated from College of William and Mary 1762. Admitted to the bar 1767. Served in Virginia House of Burgesses 1769–75; member of colony's committee of correspondence. Published *Summary View of the Rights of British America* 1774. Elected to Continental Congress 1775. Drafted Declaration of Independence June 1776. Member of Virginia legislature 1776–79. Governor of Virginia 1779–81. Returned to Congress 1783. Minister to France 1785–89. Drafted Virginia Statute of Religious Freedom 1786. Published *Notes on the State of Virginia* 1785. Secretary of State under President Washington 1790–93. Elected Vice-President 1796. Elected third U.S. President 1800 and served two terms 1801–9. Authorized Louisiana Purchase of 1803 and Lewis and Clark expedition. Founded University of Virginia 1819 and served as first rector. President of American Philosophical Society 1797–1815. Died at Virginia home, Monticello, on July 4, 1826.

LAFAYETTE, MARQUIS DE (1757–1834), soldier. Born in Chavaniac, France, September 6, 1757. Began military career at age of fifteen. Received commission in Continental Army and came to America 1777.

Served under General Washington 1777–78. Returned to France January 1779 to seek aid for American war. Returned to America three months later and resumed military responsibilities, remaining in army until defeat of British at Yorktown 1781. Returned to France 1782. Played leading role in early stages of French Revolution 1789–91. One of the drafters of the *Declaration of the Rights of Man and of the Citizen*. Commanded Paris militia 1789–91. Appointed lieutenant general for the war between France and Austria. Suspended by the Constituent Assembly, he was a prisoner of the Austrian-Prussian forces for five years, 1792–97. Returned to France 1799. Retired from public life until elected to Chamber of Deputies 1815; served until 1824, when he went to the U.S. for a visit at the invitation of President Monroe. Returned to Chamber of Deputies 1827–34. Commanded national guard during Revolution of 1830. He died in Paris on May 20, 1834.

LEE, RICHARD HENRY (1732–94), public official. Born in Westmoreland County, Virginia, January 20, 1732. Graduated from Academy of Wakefield in Yorkshire, England, 1751. Elected to Virginia House of Burgesses 1758. In 1773 he cooperated with Thomas Jefferson and Patrick Henry to initiate committees of correspondence. Elected to Continental Congress 1774. Introduced resolution calling for independence from Britain June 1776. Served in Virginia legislature 1780–84. Member of Continental Congress 1784–87. Opposed ratification of new Constitution. Elected to U.S. Senate, where he served until 1792. Died at Stratford, Virginia, on June 19, 1794.

LINCOLN, ABRAHAM (1809–65), sixteenth President of the U.S. Born near Hodgenville, Kentucky, February 12, 1809. Settled in Illinois 1830. Despite lack of formal schooling, was admitted to the bar 1836. Member of state legislature 1834–41. Elected to one term in U.S. House of Representatives 1846. His sagging political career revived by opposition to Kansas-Nebraska Bill of 1854 and to policies of Illinois senator Stephen A. Douglas. Engaged in series of debates with Douglas on the slavery issue during his campaign for Douglas's Senate seat, but lost the election, 1858. Elected President on Republican Party ticket 1860. His goal during the Civil War was to save the Union, not free the slaves. Issued Emancipation Proclamation of 1863 as a war measure. Re-elected to the presidency on coalition ticket 1864. On April 14, 1865, five days after Lee's surrender at Appomattox, Lincoln was assassinated by John Wilkes Booth at Ford's Theater in Washington, D.C.

LOCKE, JOHN (1632–1704), philosopher. Born in Somersetshire, England, August 29, 1632. Graduated from Oxford 1656 and remained there as an instructor. Had wide-ranging interests in natural sciences, medicine, philosophy, and political theory. Settled in London 1667 as personal physician and adviser to the Chancellor of the Exchequer, a position he held for sixteen years. Wrote, over period of twenty years, his *Essay Concerning Human Understanding,* finally published 1690. Lived in France 1675–79. Coming under royal disfavor, he went to Holland 1683, returning 1689 after the "Glorious Revolution." Published *Letter Concerning Toleration* 1689, *Two Treatises on Civil Government* 1690. Retired to Essex 1691 to continue his writing. Served on commission on trade and plantations 1696–1700. Lived in retirement at Essex until his death there on October 28, 1704.

MADISON, JAMES (1751–1836), fourth President of the U.S. Born in Port Conway, Virginia, March 16, 1751. Graduated from College of New Jersey (now Princeton) 1770. Elected to Virginia Constitutional Convention 1776. Served in Continental Congress 1779–83. Member of Virginia House of Delegates 1784–86. Delegate to Annapolis Convention of 1786 and to Constitutional Convention of 1787. His notes on the latter are the single most important source of information on the proceedings. Co-authored the *Federalist Papers* of 1788 with Alexander Hamilton and John Jay. Elected to U.S. House of Representatives 1789 and served until 1797. Co-author with Jefferson of Virginia and Kentucky Resolves (1798) protesting Alien and Sedition Acts. Secretary of State under Jefferson 1801–9. Served two terms as President 1809–17. Retired to Montpelier, Virginia, 1817. Member of Virginia Constitutional Convention 1829. Rector of University of Virginia from 1826 until his death at Montpelier on June 28, 1836.

MARSHALL, JOHN (1755–1835), Chief Justice of the U.S. Supreme Court. Born in Fauquier County, Virginia, September 24, 1755. Served in colony's militia and in Continental Army during revolutionary war. Admitted to the bar 1780. Member of Virginia legislature 1782–88. Served with Elbridge Gerry and Charles C. Pinckney as a commissioner to France 1797–98. Elected to U.S. House of Representatives 1799. Named Secretary of State by President John Adams in 1800 and appointed Chief Justice of the U.S. Supreme Court in 1801. His tenure on the court served to make it an effective force for a strong national government. Among most notable opinions were *Marbury* v. *Madison*

(1803), *Dartmouth College* v. *Woodward* (1819), *M'Culloch* v. *Maryland* (1819). He died in Philadelphia on July 6, 1835.

MASON, GEORGE (1725–92), public official. Born in Fairfax County, Virginia, in 1725. Little formal education. Treasurer of the Ohio Company 1752–73; planter and large landholder. Elected to one term in Virginia House of Burgesses 1758. Promoted colonial rights against British rule. Drafted Virginia Constitution and Virginia Bill of Rights of 1776. Member of state legislature 1776–88. Delegate to Constitutional Convention of 1787, but opposed ratification of new Constitution. Refused thereafter to serve in public office. Died at his Gunston Hall plantation on October 7, 1792.

MONTESQUIEU, CHARLES DE (1689–1755), jurist and political theorist. Born in La Brède, France, near Bordeaux, January 18, 1689. Educated at the College of the Oratorians in Juilly. Prepared for a career in law in Bordeaux 1705–8 but had greater interest in literature. Published the *Persian Letters* 1721. Settled in Paris 1726. Elected to French Academy 1728. Toured Europe for several years to make comparative study of societies and institutions. Returned to live at La Brède. Published *Spirit of Laws* 1748. Died in Paris on February 10, 1755.

PAINE, THOMAS (1737–1809), political reformer. Born in Thetford, England, January 29, 1737. Emigrated to Philadelphia 1774. Wrote extremely successful tract, *Common Sense* (1776). During service in Continental Army 1776–77 wrote series of pamphlets under over-all title of *The Crisis*. Secretary of the committee on foreign affairs for Continental Congress 1777–79. Clerk of Pennsylvania Assembly 1779–81. With John Laurens on a mission to France to seek aid for the Revolution. Returned to Europe 1787. Published *The Rights of Man* (1791–92) as response to Edmund Burke's *Reflections on the French Revolution.* Made an honorary French citizen, he was elected to Revolutionary Convention 1792. Imprisoned in Paris 1793–94. Published *The Age of Reason* 1794–96. Returned to U.S. in 1802 and lived in relative obscurity until his death in New York City on June 8, 1809.

PENDLETON, EDMUND (1721–1803), public official. Born in Caroline County, Virginia, September 9, 1721. Admitted to the bar 1742. Elected to House of Burgesses 1752 and served there until his death. A political foe of Patrick Henry, he nevertheless became a member of

Virginia's committee of correspondence 1773. Member of first Continental Congress 1774–75. Headed Virginia's revolutionary government 1775–76. Assisted in reworking of the colony's laws when independence was declared. First speaker of state House of Representatives. President of state's Supreme Court of Appeals 1779–1803. President of Virginia ratifying convention 1788 and a strong proponent of new Constitution. Declining any federal posts, he continued to serve Virginia until his death in Caroline County on October 26, 1803.

PETITION OF RIGHT. A legal assertion of rights by a British subject against the Crown. Best known is Parliamentary Petition of 1628 against Charles I, alleging breach of laws.

RESOLUTION OF INDEPENDENCE. Introduced by Richard Henry Lee to second Continental Congress on June 7, 1776, and approved by the Congress on July 2. Led to naming of drafting committees that produced Declaration of Independence and Articles of Confederation.

SMITH, WILLIAM (1727–1803), educator and clergyman. Born in Aberdeen, Scotland, September 7, 1727. Emigrated to America 1751. Involved in planning King's College (now Columbia) in New York City. Returned to England to be ordained priest of Anglican Church. Taught at College and Academy of Philadelphia 1754–55; provost of college 1755–79. Helped establish schools throughout Pennsylvania, especially among German residents. Edited *American Magazine and Monthly Chronicle* 1757–58. Served as pastor of Anglican parish at Oxford, Pennsylvania, 1766–77. Suspected of being a Loyalist during the Revolution, he moved to Barbados 1777–78. Founder (1782) and first president of Washington College, Chestertown, Maryland. Returned to his position as provost at College of Philadelphia 1789. Retired 1791 when school was absorbed by the new University of Pennsylvania. He died in Philadelphia on May 14, 1803.

STORY, JOSEPH (1779–1845), Associate Justice of U.S. Supreme Court. Born in Marblehead, Massachusetts, September 18, 1779. Graduated from Harvard 1798. Admitted to the bar 1801. Served in state legislature 1805–7, 1810–11, and in U.S. House of Representatives 1808–9. Appointed by President Madison to U.S. Supreme Court 1811, where Story joined Chief Justice Marshall as proponent of a strong federal government. Professor of law at Harvard 1829–45 while remaining on the bench. Published *Commentaries* on the Constitution and on law 1833–45. He died in Cambridge, Massachusetts, on September 10, 1845.

TANEY, ROGER BROOKE (1777–1864), Chief Justice of the U.S. Supreme Court. Born in Calvert County, Maryland, March 17, 1777. Graduated from Dickinson College 1795. Admitted to the bar 1799. Active in state politics as a Federalist until 1823, when he joined the Democratic Party of Andrew Jackson. Maryland Attorney General 1827–31. Became U.S. Attorney General 1831. Served as Secretary of the Treasury beginning September 1833, but U.S. Senate refused to confirm his appointment. Returned to law practice 1835. Senate also refused confirmation of appointment as Associate Justice of U.S. Supreme Court in 1835, but in the following year he was confirmed as Chief Justice. He did not fulfill his opponents' fears that he would undo the work of the Marshall Court with its strong nationalism. Most controversial decision was his opinion in *Dred Scott* v. *Sandford* case (1857), denying Congress the power to ban slavery in the territories. He died in Washington, D.C., on October 12, 1864.

TUCKER, THOMAS TUDOR (1745–1828), public official. Born on the island of Bermuda in 1745. Medical degree from the University of Edinburgh. Settled in South Carolina. Served as surgeon in Continental Army during the Revolution. Member of Continental Congress 1787–88. Served in U.S. House of Representatives 1789–93. Appointed Treasurer of the U.S. by President Jefferson 1801 and remained in the post until his death in 1828.

VIRGINIA DECLARATION OF RIGHTS. Statement on individual rights and the nature of government written by George Mason, a member of the drafting committee of Virginia Constitutional Convention of 1776. Adopted June 12, 1776, prior to acceptance of the new state Constitution. Served as model for U.S. Bill of Rights (1791) and French Declaration of the Rights of Man and of the Citizen (1791).

WASHINGTON, GEORGE (1732–99), first President of the U.S. Born in Westmoreland County, Virginia, February 22, 1732. With little formal education, he became a surveyor in 1747. Inherited Mount Vernon estate in 1751. Commissioned lieutenant colonel of a Virginia regiment 1754. Built Fort Necessity near present-day Pittsburgh, which he was forced to surrender to the French at start of French and Indian War. Was present at Braddock's defeat in 1755. As commander of Virginia forces in 1758 he aided in capture of Fort Duquesne. Served in Virginia House of Burgesses 1759–74; elected to Continental Congress 1774. Chosen commander-in-chief of Continental Army 1775, in which capacity he served until the end of the revolutionary war. Delegate to Annapolis Convention 1786. Chairman of Constitutional Convention of 1787. Elected President 1789 and re-elected 1792. Refusing a third term, he published "Farewell Address" in 1796 and the following year retired to Mount Vernon. Appointed commanding general of the army in 1798 by President John Adams, in face of threatened war with France. He died at Mount Vernon on December 14, 1799.

WILSON, JAMES (1742–98), Associate Justice of the U.S. Supreme Court. Born in Fifeshire, Scotland, September 14, 1742. Educated at St. Andrew's and Edinburgh universities. Emigrated to America and settled in Philadelphia 1765. Admitted to the bar 1767. Settled in Carlisle, Pennsylvania, and gained a reputation as an outstanding lawyer and political theorist. Promoted the colonial cause against British authority. Elected to the first Continental Congress 1774. Published the same year a revised version of his *Considerations on the Nature and Extent of the Legislative Authority of the British Parliament*. A member of the second Continental Congress, he was a signer of the Declaration of Independence. Served again in Congress 1782–83, 1785–87. A delegate to the Constitutional Convention of 1787, he played a pivotal role in designing the Constitution to reflect a balance of national and local authority, believing that the new government derived its powers from the people, not the states. Led the struggle for ratification of the new Constitution in Pennsylvania. Played a leading role in the writing of a new state constitution 1790. Appointed to the new U.S. Supreme Court by President Washington 1789; the same year became the first professor of law at the College of Philadelphia. His series of lectures on law in 1790 enunciated a nationalist position on the Constitution. He died in Edenton, North Carolina, on August 21, 1798.

Index